A Handbook on the GATS Agreement

The General Agreement on Trade in Services (GATS) is a relatively new agreement. It entered into force in January 1995 as a result of the Uruguay Round negotiations to provide for the extension of the multilateral trading system to services.

This handbook aims to provides a better understanding of GATS and the challenges and opportunities of the ongoing negotiations. For users who are familiar with the General Agreement on Tariffs and Trade (GATT), similarities and differences are pointed out where relevant. Likewise, for users who are familiar with the balance-of-payments definition of 'trade', departures from the Agreement's coverage are explained.

To stimulate further thinking about core concepts and implications of the Agreement, several text boxes have been inserted to provide 'Food for thought'.

A Handbook on the GATS Agreement

A WTO Secretariat Publication
Prepared by the WTO Trade in Services Division

CAMBRIDGE
UNIVERSITY PRESS

CAMBRIDGE UNIVERSITY PRESS
Cambridge, New York, Melbourne, Madrid, Cape Town, Singapore,
São Paulo, Delhi, Dubai, Tokyo

Cambridge University Press
The Edinburgh Building, Cambridge CB2 8RU, UK

Published in the United States of America by Cambridge University Press, New York

www.cambridge.org
Information on this title: www.cambridge.org/9780521615679

© World Trade Organization 2005

This publication is in copyright. Subject to statutory exception
and to the provisions of relevant collective licensing agreements,
no reproduction of any part may take place without the written
permission of Cambridge University Press.

First published 2005

A catalogue record for this publication is available from the British Library

ISBN 978-0-521-85071-1 Hardback
ISBN 978-0-521-61567-9 Paperback

Cambridge University Press has no responsibility for the persistence or
accuracy of URLs for external or third-party internet websites referred to in
this publication, and does not guarantee that any content on such websites is,
or will remain, accurate or appropriate. Information regarding prices, travel
timetables and other factual information given in this work are correct at
the time of first printing but Cambridge University Press does not guarantee
the accuracy of such information thereafter.

Transferred to digital printing 2009

CONTENTS

PREFACE

The primary purpose of this handbook is to explain the General Agreement on Trade in Services to an interested person with little or no knowledge of the agreement. However, with its detailed content, it can also serve as a useful guide for experienced practitioners working in various services sectors. Special thanks are addressed to those in the Trade in Services Division and in the Information and Media Relations Division who have assisted in researching, drafting and editing this publication.

Hamid Mamdouh
Director
Trade in Services Division
World Trade Organization

DISCLAIMER

The WTO Secretariat has prepared this handbook for the General Agreement on Trade in Services to assist public understanding of the GATS. It is not intended to provide a legal interpretation of the GATS.

INTRODUCTION

The General Agreement on Trade in Services (GATS) is a relatively new agreement. It entered into force in January 1995 as a result of the Uruguay Round negotiations to provide for the extension of the multilateral trading system to services. With a view to achieving a progressively higher level of liberalization, pursuant to Article XIX of the GATS, WTO Members are committed to entering into further rounds of services negotiations. The first such round started in January 2000.

All Members of the WTO are signatories to the GATS and have to assume the resulting obligations. So, regardless of their countries' policy stances, trade officials need to be familiar with this agreement and its implications for trade and development. These implications may be far more significant than available trade data suggest.

Hopefully, these materials will contribute to a better understanding of the GATS and the challenges and opportunities of the ongoing negotiations. For users who are familiar with the General Agreement on Tariffs and Trade (GATT), similarities and differences will be pointed out where relevant. Likewise, for users who are familiar with the balance-of-payments definition of "trade", departures from the Agreement's coverage will be explained. Whenever indicated, it is recommended to supplement these materials with documents available on the WTO website (www.wto.org).

To stimulate further thinking about core concepts and implications of the Agreement, several boxes have been inserted to provide "Food for thought".

1

BASIC PURPOSE AND CONCEPTS

HISTORICAL BACKGROUND

The General Agreement on Trade in Services (GATS) is the first multilateral trade agreement to cover trade in services. Its creation was one of the major achievements of the Uruguay Round of trade negotiations held from 1986 to 1993. This was almost half a century after the entry into force of the General Agreement on Tariffs and Trade (GATT) of 1947, the GATS counterpart in merchandise trade.

The need for a trade agreement in services has long been questioned. Large segments of the services economy, from hotels and restaurants to personal services, have traditionally been considered as domestic activities that do not lend themselves to the application of trade policy concepts and instruments. Other sectors, from rail transport to telecommunications, have been viewed as classical domains of government ownership and control, given their infrastructural importance and the perceived existence, in some cases, of natural monopoly situations. A third important group of sectors, including health, education and basic insurance services, are considered in many countries to be governmental responsibilities, given their importance for social integration and regional cohesion, which should be tightly regulated and not be left to the rough and tumble of markets.

Nevertheless, some services sectors, in particular international finance and maritime transport, have been largely open for centuries – as the natural complements to merchandise trade. Other large sectors have undergone fundamental technical and regulatory changes in recent decades, opening them to private commercial participation and reducing, even eliminating, existing barriers to entry. The emergence of the Internet has helped to create a range of internationally tradeable product variants – from e-banking to tele-health and distance learning – that were unknown only two decades ago, and has removed distance-related barriers to trade that had disadvantaged suppliers and users in remote locations (relevant areas include professional services such as software development, consultancy and advisory services, etc.). A growing number of governments has gradually exposed previous monopoly domains to competition; telecommunication is a case in point.

This reflects a basic change in attitudes. The traditional framework of public service increasingly proved inappropriate for operating some of the most dynamic and innovative segments of the economy, and governments apparently lacked the entrepreneurial spirit and financial resources to exploit fully existing growth potential.

Services have recently become the most dynamic segment of international trade. Since 1980 world services trade has grown faster, albeit from a relatively modest basis, than merchandise flows. Defying widespread misconceptions, developing countries have strongly participated in that growth. Between 1990 and 2000 their services exports, consisting mainly of tourism and travel services, grew 3 per cent more rapidly per annum, on a balance-of-payments basis, than developed countries' exports.

Given the continued momentum of world services trade, the need for internationally recognized rules became increasingly pressing.

BASIC PURPOSE

As stated in its Preamble, the GATS is intended to contribute to trade expansion "under conditions of transparency and progressive liberalization and as a means of promoting the economic growth of all trading partners and the development of developing countries". Trade expansion is thus not seen as an end in itself, as some critical voices allege, but as an instrument to promote growth and development. The link with development is further reinforced by explicit references in the Preamble to the objective of increasing participation of developing countries in services trade and to the special economic situation and the development, trade and financial needs of the least developed countries.

The GATS' contribution to world services trade rests on two main pillars: (a) ensuring increased transparency and predictability of relevant rules and regulations, and (b) promoting progressive liberalization through successive rounds of negotiations. Within the framework of the Agreement, the latter concept is tantamount to improving market access and extending national treatment to foreign services and service suppliers across an increasing range of sectors. It does not, however, entail deregulation. Rather, the Agreement explicitly recognizes the right of governments to regulate and to introduce new regulations in order to meet national policy objectives, and the particular need of developing countries to exercise this right.

To a considerable degree, the drafters of the GATS took inspiration from the GATT and used terms and concepts that had already been tested for decades in merchandise trade. These include the principles of most-favoured-nation (MFN) treatment and national treatment. Comparable to its status under the GATT, MFN treatment – the obligation not to discriminate between fellow WTO Members – is an unconditional obligation, which applies across all services covered by GATS. The tariff schedules under the GATT, in which countries bind their tariff concessions on merchandise imports, find their equivalent in schedules of specific commitments which define the relevant trade conditions for services.

Reflecting peculiarities of services trade, however, there are also notable differences in scope and content between the two agreements.

(a) Unlike the GATT, the GATS covers measures affecting both the product (service) and the supplier.

(b) The definition of services trade covers not only cross-border supply, but three additional forms of transaction ("modes of supply").

(c) While quota-free entry ("market access") and national treatment are generally applicable obligations under the GATT, they apply under the GATS on a sector-by-sector basis and only to the extent that no qualifications ("limitations") have been scheduled.

Food for thought

(i) In your opinion, why was the GATS necessary?

(ii) How does the purpose of the GATS fit with your national development objectives?

Possible reply

(i) Increasing economic importance of services production and trade as a result of: technical progress, government retrenchment (privatization, commercialization of important services sectors), increased reliance on market forces in general.

(ii) Role of services, in particular in infrastructurally relevant areas (finance, communication, transport, etc.), as determinants of overall economic efficiency.

(iii) Positive impact of multilateral access guarantees on inflows of investment, skills and expertise.

(iv) Possibility of reaping economies of scale and scope within an internationally open services environment.

DEFINITION OF SERVICES TRADE AND MODES OF SUPPLY

The definition of services trade under the GATS is four-pronged, depending on the territorial presence of the supplier and the consumer at the time of the transaction. Pursuant to Article I:2, the GATS covers services supplied

(a) from the territory of one Member into the territory of any other Member (mode 1 – cross-border trade);

(b) in the territory of one Member to the service consumer of any other Member (mode 2 – consumption abroad);

(c) by a service supplier of one Member, through commercial presence, in the territory of any other Member (mode 3 – commercial presence); and

---

EXAMPLES OF THE FOUR MODES OF SUPPLY (FROM THE PERSPECTIVE OF AN "IMPORTING" COUNTRY A)

Mode 1: cross-border

A user in country A receives services from abroad through its telecommunications or postal infrastructure. Such supplies may include consultancy or market research reports, tele-medical advice, distance training or architectural drawings.

Mode 2: consumption abroad

Nationals of A have moved abroad as tourists, students or patients to consume the respective services.

Mode 3: commercial presence

The service is provided within A by a locally established affiliate, subsidiary or representative office of a foreign-owned and -controlled company (bank, hotel group, construction company, etc.).

Mode 4: movement of natural persons

A foreign national provides a service within A as an independent supplier (e.g. consultant, health worker) or employee of a service supplier (e.g. consultancy firm, hospital, construction company).

Figure 1

(d) by a service supplier of one Member, through the presence of natural persons of a Member in the territory of any other Member (mode 4 – presence of natural persons).

Figure 1 gives examples of the four modes of supply.

The above definition is significantly broader than the balance-of-payments (BOP) concept of services trade. While the BOP focuses on residency rather than nationality – that is a service is being exported if it is traded between residents and non-residents – certain transactions falling under the GATS, in particular in the case of mode 3, typically involve only residents of the country concerned.

Commercial linkages may exist among all four modes of supply. For example, a foreign company established under mode 3 in country A may employ nationals from country B (mode 4) to export services cross-border into countries B, C and so on. Similarly, business visits into A (mode 4) may prove necessary to complement cross-border supplies into that country (mode 1) or to upgrade the capacity of a locally established office (mode 3).

SCOPE AND APPLICATION

Article I:1 stipulates that the GATS applies to measures taken by Members affecting trade in services. It does not matter in this context whether a measure is taken at central, regional or local government level, or by non-governmental bodies exercising delegated powers. The relevant definition covers any measure, contained in Article XXVIII,

> whether in the form of a law, regulation, rule, procedure, decision, administrative action, or any other form, . . . in respect of:
>
> (i) the purchase, payment or use of a service;
>
> (ii) the access to and use of, in connection with the supply of a service, services which are required by those Members to be offered to the public generally;
>
> (iii) the presence, including commercial presence, of persons of a Member for the supply of a service in the territory of another Member.

This definition is significantly broader than what governmental officials in trade-related areas may expect. It is thus important to familiarize staff at all levels with basic concepts of the GATS to prevent them from acting, unintentionally, in contravention of obligations under the Agreement and to enable them to negotiate effectively with trading partners.

For purposes of structuring their commitments, WTO Members have generally used a classification system comprising twelve core service sectors:

> business services (including professional services and computer services)
> communication services
> construction and related engineering services
> distribution services
> educational services
> environmental services
> financial services (including insurance and banking)
> health-related and social services
> tourism and travel-related services
> recreational, cultural and sporting services
> transport services
> other services not included elsewhere

These sectors are further subdivided into a total of some 160 sub-sectors. Under this classification system, any service sector may be included in a Member's schedule of commitments with specific market access and national treatment obligations. Each WTO Member has submitted such a schedule under the GATS.

There is only one sector-specific exception to the Agreement's otherwise comprehensive coverage. Under the GATS Annex on Air Transport Services, only measures affecting aircraft repair and maintenance services, the selling and marketing of air transport services, and computer reservation system (CRS) services have been included. Measures affecting air traffic rights and directly related services are excluded. This exclusion is subject to periodic review.

Another blanket exemption applies to "services supplied in the exercise of governmental authority" (Article I:3b). The relevant definition specifies that these services are "supplied neither on a commercial basis, nor in competition with one or more service suppliers" (Article I:3c). Typical examples may include police, fire protection, monetary policy operations, mandatory social security, and tax and customs administration.

Despite its broad coverage, the GATS does not compromise Members' ability to regulate for national policy purposes. Issues related to domestic regulation will be further discussed in Chapter 3.

GENERAL TRANSPARENCY AND OTHER "GOOD GOVERNANCE" OBLIGATIONS

Sufficient information about potentially relevant rules and regulations is critical to the effective implementation of an agreement. Article III ensures of the GATS Agreement that Members publish promptly all measures pertaining to or affecting the operation of the GATS. Moreover, there is an obligation to notify the Council for Trade in Services at least annually of all legal or regulatory changes that significantly affect trade in sectors where specific commitments have been made. Members are also required to establish enquiry points which provide specific information to other Members upon request. However, there is no requirement to disclose confidential information (Article III *bis*).

Given strong government involvement in many service markets – for various reasons, including social policy objectives or the existence of natural monopolies – the Agreement seeks to ensure that relevant measures do not undermine general obligations, such as MFN treatment or specific commitments in individual sectors. Thus, each Member is required to ensure, in sectors where commitments exist, that measures of general application are administered impartially and in a reasonable and objective manner (Article VI:1). Service suppliers in all sectors must be able to use national tribunals or procedures in order to challenge administrative decisions affecting services trade (Article VI:2a).

Food for thought
Give examples of policies that are currently in place to support your government's transparency commitments.

Possible reply
Publication of relevant laws and regulations in official journals, government gazettes and so on. Operation of information centres. Consultations with industry, trade and consumer associations.

MOST-FAVOURED-NATION TREATMENT

The most-favoured-nation (MFN) principle is a cornerstone of the multilateral trading system conceived after World War II. It seeks to replace the frictions and distortions of power-based (bilateral) policies with the guarantees of a rules-based framework where trading rights do not depend on the individual participants' economic or political clout. Rather, the best access conditions that have been conceded to one country must automatically be extended to all other participants in the system. This allows everybody to benefit, without additional negotiating effort, from concessions that may have been agreed between large trading partners with much negotiating leverage.

In the context of the GATS, the MFN obligation (Article II) is applicable to any measure that affects trade in services in any sector falling under the Agreement, whether specific commitments have been made or not. Exemptions could have been sought at the time of the acceptance of the Agreement (for acceding countries: date of accession). They are contained in country-specific lists, and their duration must not exceed ten years in principle.

CONDITIONAL GRANTING OF MARKET ACCESS AND NATIONAL TREATMENT

The GATS is a very flexible agreement that allows each Member to adjust the conditions of market entry and participation to its sector-specific objectives and constraints. Two sets of legal obligations – governing, respectively, market access and national treatment – are relevant in this context. As already noted, Members are free to designate the sectors, and list them in their schedules of commitments, in which they assume such obligations with regard to the four modes of supply. Moreover, limitations may be attached to commitments in order to reserve the right to operate measures inconsistent with full market access and/or national treatment.

The *market access* provisions of GATS, laid down in Article XVI, cover six types of restrictions that must not be maintained in the absence of limitations. The restrictions relate to

- (a) the number of service suppliers
- (b) the value of service transactions or assets
- (c) the number of operations or quantity of output
- (d) the number of natural persons supplying a service
- (e) the type of legal entity or joint venture
- (f) the participation of foreign capital

These measures, except for (e) and (f), are not necessarily discriminatory, that is they may affect national as well as foreign services or service suppliers.

National treatment (Article XVII) implies the absence of all discriminatory measures that may modify the conditions of competition to the detriment of foreign services or service suppliers. Again, limitations may be listed to provide cover for inconsistent measures, such as discriminatory subsidies and tax measures, residency requirements and so on. It is for the individual Member to ensure that all potentially relevant measures are listed; Article XVII does not contain a typology comparable with that of Article XVI. (Examples of frequently scheduled national treatment restrictions are given in Attachment 1 to document S/L/92.) The national treatment obligation applies regardless of whether foreign services and suppliers are treated in a formally identical way to their national counterpart. What matters is that they are granted equal opportunities to compete.

The purpose of commitments, comparable to tariff concessions under GATT, is to ensure stability and predictability of trading conditions. However, commitments are not a straitjacket. They may be renegotiated against compensation of affected trading partners (Article XXI), and there are special provisions that allow for flexible responses, despite existing commitments, in specified circumstances. Under Article XIV, for example, Members may take measures necessary for certain overriding policy concerns, including the protection of public morals or the protection of human, animal or plant life or health. However, such measures must not lead to arbitrary or unjustifiable discrimination or constitute a disguised restriction to trade. If essential security interests are at stake, Article XIV *bis* provides cover. Article XII allows for the introduction of temporary restrictions to safeguard the balance of payments; and a so-called prudential carve-out in financial services permits Members to take measures in order, *inter alia*, to ensure the integrity and stability of their financial system (Annex on Financial Services, para. 2).

Commitments must not necessarily be complied with from the date of entry into force of a schedule. Rather, Members may specify in relevant part(s) of their schedule a timeframe for implementation. Such "pre-commitments" are as legally valid as any other commitment.

Food for thought
Imagine that your country intended to schedule the following services: telecommunications, banking and rail transport.
 (i) What could be an example of a market access restriction in these sectors?
(ii) What could be an example of a national treatment restriction?

Possible reply
 (i) Existence of exclusive or monopoly operators. Prescribed forms of legal incorporation (e.g. joint stock companies). Quantitative restrictions on presence of natural persons.
(ii) Restrictions on foreigners' participation in company boards. Prohibition of foreign land ownership. Discriminatory minimum capital or minimum reserve requirements.

2

MAIN BUILDING BLOCKS: AGREEMENT, ANNEXES AND SCHEDULES

THE BASIC STRUCTURE OF THE GATS

The GATS forms part of the Marrakesh Agreement Establishing the World Trade Organization. It establishes a rules-based framework for international trade in services, specifies the obligations of Members within that framework, and delineates a legal structure to ensure compliance. The Marrakesh Agreement includes two other multilateral agreements – GATT 1994, and the Agreement on Trade-Related Aspects of Intellectual Property Rights (TRIPS) – as well as a few plurilateral agreements. Of these, the Agreement on Government Procurement is also of relevance to trade in services.

The GATS consists of the text of the Agreement (a Preamble, 29 Articles arranged in six Parts (see Figure 2), and various Annexes) and a schedule of commitments for each WTO Member.

THE TEXT OF THE AGREEMENT

Preamble
The Preamble states the main intentions that inspired the drafting of the Agreement. These include the concept of trade expansion as a means of promoting growth and development and the objective of progressive trade liberalization through successive rounds of negotiations. Further, the Preamble explicitly confirms the right of Members to regulate, and to introduce new regulations, to meet national policy objectives. The two final considerations refer to the objective of facilitating the increasing participation of developing countries in world services trade as well as to the special economic situation of least-developed countries and their development, trade and financial needs.

A framework of principles
The main body of the Agreement outlines Members' obligations concerning their use of measures (laws, rules, regulations, procedures, decisions or administrative actions) affecting trade in services. These principles will be discussed further in the next three sections.

Annexes covering sector- or policy-related issues
Annex on Article II Exemptions. The Annex lays downs the conditions under which Members could have been exempted, at the entry into force of the Agreement (for

newly acceding Members: date of accession), from the basic obligation to MFN treatment. Such exemptions should not exceed ten years in principle.

Annex on Movement of Natural Persons. The Annex clarifies that the scope of the GATS does not extend to measures affecting persons seeking access to the employment market or to measures governing citizenship, residence or permanent employment. The right of Members to control entry or temporary stay through visa requirements or other means remains unaffected.

Annex on Air Transport Services. International air transport services are for the most part governed by arrangements negotiated under the Chicago Convention. The Annex thus excludes from the scope of GATS measures affecting air traffic rights and services directly related to their exercise. By the same token, it provides that measures affecting aircraft repair and maintenance services, the selling and marketing of air transport services, and computer reservation systems (CRS) services are covered. Further, there is a clause requiring the Council for Trade in Services to review at least every five years developments in air transport with a view to considering the possible extension of GATS to this sector.

Annex on Financial Services. Given the crucial role of the financial sector for overall economic stability, governments throughout the world closely regulate banks, insurance companies and other financial service providers. The Annex is intended mainly to clarify some core GATS provisions as they apply to financial services. One of the central elements is the so-called "prudential carve-out". In essence, it confirms "notwithstanding any other provisions of the Agreement" that WTO Members are free to take prudential measures to protect investors, depositors, policy holders or persons to whom a fiduciary duty is owed by a financial service supplier, or to ensure the integrity and stability of the financial system. The Annex also specifies the scope of the governmental service exception in Article I:3b regarding financial services and contains various definitions relevant to the sector.

Annex on Telecommunications. The Annex takes into account the particular role of telecommunications as a transport medium in virtually all sectors, and delineates the conditions governing access to and use of public telecommunications networks and services. Whenever a sector is listed in a Member's schedule, all foreign suppliers in that sector must be treated on a "reasonable and non-discriminatory" basis in their use of all public telecommunications services, such as the telephone, leased lines and data transmission.

Among other things, the Annex spells out the rights of foreign telecommunication users in a committed sector. These include the right to buy or lease the equipment needed to connect to the public network, to connect private circuits with the public system or with other circuits, and to use the public network to transmit information. The Annex also allows Members to place reasonable conditions on access and use in specific circumstances. Developing countries may depart from Annex obligations if necessary to strengthen the domestic infrastructure and service capacity, so long as such conditions are specified in the GATS schedule. Other provisions seek to

---

INDIVIDUAL PROVISIONS OF THE GATS

Part I (Article I)
Outlines the scope of the Agreement, its sectoral coverage and defines trade in services.

Part II (Articles II–XV)
Sets out Members' general obligations which apply either conditionally – that is contingent on the existence of specific commitments – or unconditionally to all sectors.

Part III (Articles XVI–XVIII)
Specifies the scope of the specific commitments governing market access and national treatment and any additional commitments which Members may undertake in scheduled sectors.

Part IV (Articles XIX–XXI)
Provides a framework for future services rounds, and specifies the structure of schedules and the procedures governing modification or withdrawal of commitments.

Part V (Articles XXII–XXVI)
Clarifies institutional and procedural issues, including the mandate of the GATS Council for Trade in Services, and recourse to dispute settlement.

Part VI (Articles XXVII–XXIX)
Includes final provisions and definitions.

Figure 2

promote technical co-operation with and between developing countries and to lend support to international standardization to ensure compatibility and interoperability of networks and services.

Annex on Negotiations on Maritime Transport Services. The Annex provided for the continued non-application of the MFN obligation in maritime transport for those Members that have not undertaken specific commitments in this sector. Following the suspension of the negotiations on maritime transport in 1996, the Council for Trade in Services took a decision to the same effect (document S/L/24).

SCHEDULES OF SPECIFIC COMMITMENTS

Each Member had to submit a schedule detailing the commitments on market access and national treatment as well as any additional commitments it undertakes in individual sectors. The content and structure of schedules are discussed further in the sections "Specific commitments" and "How schedules are structured", below.

UNCONDITIONAL GENERAL OBLIGATIONS

Each Member has to respect certain general obligations that apply regardless of the existence of specific commitments. These include MFN treatment (Article II), some basic transparency provisions (Article III), the availability of legal remedies (Article VI:2), compliance of monopolies and exclusive providers with the MFN obligation (Article VII:1), consultations on business practices (Article IX) and consultations on subsidies that affect trade (Article XV:2). In several cases the same article contains both unconditional and conditional obligations.

MOST-FAVOURED-NATION TREATMENT

As already mentioned in Chapter 1 under "Most-favoured-nation treatment", the MFN principle applies across all sectors and to all Members. However, under the Annex on Article II Exemptions, there is a possibility for Members, at the time of entry into force of the Agreement (or date of accession), to seek exemptions not exceeding a period of ten years in principle. More than eighty Members currently maintain such exemptions, which are mostly intended to cover trade preferences on a regional basis. The sectors predominantly concerned are road transport and audiovisual services, followed by maritime transport and banking services.

TRANSPARENCY

Under Article III each Member is required to publish promptly "all relevant measures of general application" that affect operation of the Agreement. Members must also notify the Council for Trade in Services of new or changed laws, regulations or administrative guidelines that significantly affect trade in sectors subject to specific commitments. These transparency obligations are particularly relevant in the services area where the role of regulation – as a trade protective instrument and/or as a domestic policy tool – tends to feature more prominently than in most other sectors of the economy.

Members also have a general obligation to establish an enquiry point to respond to requests from other Members. Moreover, pursuant to Article IV:2, developed countries (and other Members to the extent possible) are to establish contact points to which developing country service suppliers can turn for relevant information.

DOMESTIC REGULATION

Under Article VI:2, Members are committed to operating domestic mechanisms ("judicial, arbitral or administrative tribunals or procedures") where individual service suppliers may seek legal redress. At the request of an affected supplier, these mechanisms should provide for the "prompt review of, and where justified, appropriate remedies for, administrative decisions affecting trade in service".

MONOPOLIES

Article VIII:1 requires Members to ensure that monopolies or exclusive service providers do not act in a manner inconsistent with the MFN obligation and commitments. Article XXVIII(h) specifies, in turn, that a "monopoly supplier" is an entity that has been established by the Member concerned, formally or in effect, as the sole supplier of a service.

BUSINESS PRACTICES

Article IX refers to business practices other than those falling under the monopoly-related provisions of Article VIII that restrain competition and thereby restrict trade. The Article requires each Member to consult with any other Member, upon request, with a view to eliminating such practices.

SUBSIDIES

Members that consider themselves adversely affected by subsidies granted by another Member may request consultations under Article XV:2. The latter Member is called upon to give "sympathetic consideration" to such requests.

Food for thought
  (i) Which monopolies in your economy fall within the scope of Article VIII:1 of the GATS?
 (ii) What types of subsidies could restrict or distort trade in services?

Possible reply
  (i) Voice telephony, postal services, rail and road transport, etc.
 (ii) Producer subsidies with import-substituting or export-enhancing effects.

CONDITIONAL GENERAL OBLIGATIONS

A second type of general obligations applies only to sectors listed in a Member's schedule of commitments.

DOMESTIC REGULATION

Pursuant to Article VI:1, measures of general application are to be administered "in a reasonable, objective and impartial manner". If the supply of a scheduled service is subject to authorization, Members are required to decide on applications within a reasonable period of time (Article VI:3).

Article VI:5 seeks to ensure that specific commitments are not nullified or impaired through regulatory requirements (licensing and qualification requirements, and technical standards) that are not based on objective and transparent criteria or are more burdensome than necessary to ensure quality. The scope of these provisions is limited, however, to the protection of reasonable expectations at the time of the commitment. Article VI:4 mandates negotiations to be conducted on any necessary disciplines that, taking account the above considerations, would prevent domestic regulations from constituting unnecessary barriers to trade.

Article VI:6 requires Members that have undertaken commitments on professional services to establish procedures to verify the competence of professionals of other Members.

MONOPOLIES

The GATS does not forbid the existence of monopolies or exclusive service suppliers per se (Article VIII) but, as noted above, subjects them to the unconditional MFN obligation. Moreover, under Article VIII:2, Members are enjoined to prevent such suppliers, if these are also active in sectors that are beyond the scope of their monopoly rights and covered by specific commitments, from abusing their position and act inconsistently with these commitments.

In addition, Article VIII:4 requires Members to report the formation of new monopolies to the Council for Trade in Services if the relevant sector is subject to specific commitments. The provisions of Article XXI (Modification of Schedules, see following section) apply.

PAYMENTS AND TRANSFERS

GATS Article XI requires that Members allow international transfers and payments for current transactions relating to specific commitments. It also provides that the rights and obligations of IMF Members, under the Articles of Agreement of the Fund, shall not be affected. This is subject to the proviso that capital transactions are not restricted inconsistently with specific commitments, except under Article XII (see below) or at the request of the Fund. Footnote 8 to Article XVI further circumscribes Members' ability to restrict capital movements in sectors where they have undertaken specific commitments on cross-border trade and commercial presence.

OTHER GENERAL PROVISIONS

ECONOMIC INTEGRATION AGREEMENTS

Like GATT (Article XXIV) with regard to merchandise trade, the GATS also has special provisions to exempt countries participating in integration agreements from the MFN requirement. Article V permits any WTO Member to enter into agreements to further liberalize trade in services on a bilateral or plurilateral basis, provided that the agreement has "substantial sectoral coverage" and removes substantially all discrimination between participants. Recognizing that such agreements may form part of a wider process of economic integration well beyond services trade, the Article allows the above conditions to be considered in this perspective. It also provides for their flexible application in the event of developing countries being parties to such agreements.

While economic integration agreements must be designed to facilitate trade among participants, Article V also requires that the overall level of barriers is not raised vis-à-vis non-participants in the sectors covered. Otherwise, should an agreement lead to the withdrawal of commitments, appropriate compensation must be negotiated with the Members affected. Such situations may arise, for example, if the new common regime in a sector is modelled on the previous regime of a more restrictive participating country.

Article V *bis* relates to, and provides similar legal cover for, agreements on labour markets integration. The main condition is that citizens of the countries involved are exempt from residency and work permit requirements.

RECOGNITION

Notwithstanding the MFN requirement, Article VII of the GATS provides scope for Members, when applying standards or granting licences, certificates and so on to recognize education and other qualifications that a supplier has obtained abroad. This may be done on an autonomous basis or through agreement with the country concerned. However, recognition must not be exclusive, that is other Members are to be afforded an opportunity to negotiate their accession to agreements or, in the event of autonomous recognition, to demonstrate that their requirements should be recognized as well. Article VII:3 requires that recognition not be applied as a means of discrimination between trading partners or as a disguised trade restriction.

EXCEPTIONS

Part II of the GATS (General Obligations and Disciplines) further contains exception clauses for particular circumstances. Regardless of relevant GATS obligations, Members are allowed in specified circumstances to restrict trade in the event of serious balance-of-payments difficulties (Article XII) or of health and other public policy concerns (Article XIV), or to pursue essential security interests (Article XIV *bis*).

SPECIFIC COMMITMENTS

In addition to respecting the general obligations referred to above, each Member is required to assume specific commitments relating to market access (Article XVI) and national treatment (Article XVII) in designated sectors. The relevant sectors and also any departures from the relevant obligations of Articles XVI and XVII are to be specified in the country's Schedule of Commitments.

Article XVI (Market Access) and XVII (National Treatment) commit Members to giving no less favourable treatment to foreign services and service suppliers than is provided for in the relevant columns of their Schedule. Commitments thus guarantee minimum levels of treatment, but do not prevent Members from being more open (or less discriminatory) in practice.

At first sight, it may be difficult to understand why the national treatment principle under the GATS is far more limited in scope – confined to scheduled services and subject to possible limitations – than under the GATT, where it applies across the board. The reason lies in the particular nature of services trade. Universal national treatment for goods does not necessarily imply free trade. Imports can still be controlled by tariffs which, in turn, may be bound in the country's tariff schedule. By contrast, given the impossibility of operating tariff-type measures across large segments of services trade, the general extension of national treatment in services could in practice be tantamount to guaranteeing free access.

ADDITIONAL COMMITMENTS

Members may also undertake additional commitments with respect to measures not falling under the market-access and national-treatment provisions of the Agreement. Such commitments may relate to the use of standards, qualifications or licences (Article XVIII). Additional commitments are particularly frequent in the telecommunications sector, where they have been used by some sixty Members to incorporate into their schedules certain competition and regulatory (self-)disciplines. These disciplines are laid out in a so-called Reference Paper, which an informal grouping of Members had developed during the extended negotiations in this sector.

CONTENT OF SCHEDULES

Article XX requires each Member to submit a schedule of specific commitments, but does not prescribe the sector scope or level of liberalization. Thus, while some Members have limited their commitments to less than a handful of sectors, others have listed several dozen.

Further, the Article specifies some core elements to be covered in each Member's schedule. It also provides that the schedules form "an integral part" of the GATS itself.

MODIFICATION OF SCHEDULES

Article XXI provides a framework of rules for modifying or withdrawing specific commitments. The relevant provisions may be invoked at any time after three years have elapsed from the date of entry into force of a commitment. (In the absence of emergency safeguard measures, which are still under negotiation, this waiting period is reduced to one year under certain conditions). It is thus possible for Members, subject to compensation, to adjust their commitments to new circumstances or policy considerations. At least three months' notice must be given of the proposed change. The compensation to be negotiated with affected Members consists of more liberal bindings elsewhere that "endeavour to maintain a general level of mutually advantageous commitments not less favourable to trade" than what existed before.

Application must be on an MFN basis. If the negotiations fail, Article XXI allows for arbitration. If the arbitrator finds that compensation is due, the proposed changes in commitments must not be put into effect until the compensatory adjustments are made. Should the modifying country ignore the arbitrator's findings, affected countries have the right to retaliate by withdrawing commitments.

In 1999 the Council for Trade in Services enacted detailed procedures for the modification of schedules pursuant to Article XXI (document S/L/80). Improvements to schedules, that is inscription of new sectors or removal of existing limitations, are subject to more streamlined procedures, laid down in document S/L/84.

HOW SCHEDULES ARE STRUCTURED

As noted above, the obligations of any WTO Member under GATS consist of the provisions of the Agreement and its annexes as well as the specific commitments contained in the national schedule. The schedule is a relatively complex document, more difficult to read than a tariff schedule under GATT. While a tariff schedule, in its simplest form, lists one tariff rate per product, a schedule of commitments contains at least eight entries per sector, the commitments on each market access and national treatment with regard to the four modes of supply.

The services schedule of "Arcadia", an imaginary WTO Member, displays the normal four-column format (Figure 3). While the first column specifies the sector or sub-sector concerned, the second column sets out any limitations on market access that fall within the six types of restrictions mentioned in Article XVI:2. The third column contains any limitations that Arcadia may want to place, in accordance with Article XVII, on national treatment. A final column provides the opportunity to undertake additional commitments as envisaged in Article XVIII; it is empty in this case.

Any of the entries under market access or national treatment may vary within a spectrum whose opposing ends are full commitments without limitation ("none") and full discretion to apply any measure falling under the relevant article ("unbound"). The schedule is divided into two parts. While Part I lists "horizontal commitments", that is entries that apply across all sectors that have been scheduled, Part II sets out commitments on a sector-by-sector basis.

Arcadia's horizontal commitments under mode 3, national treatment, reserve the right to deny foreign land ownership. Under mode 4, Arcadia would be able to prevent any foreigner from entering its territory to supply services, except for the specified groups of persons. Within the retailing sector, whose definitional scope

SAMPLE SCHEDULE OF COMMITMENTS: ARCADIA

Modes of supply: (1) cross-border supply; (2) consumption supply; (3) commercial presence; (4) presence of natural persons.

Sector or sub-sector	Limitations on market access	Limitations on national treatment	Additional commitments
I. HORIZONTAL COMMITMENTS			
ALL SECTORS INCLUDED IN THIS SCHEDULE	(4) Unbound, other than for (a) temporary presence, as intra-corporate transferees, of essential senior executives and specialists; and (b) presence for up to 90 days of representatives of a service provider to negotiate sales of services.	(3) Authorization is required for acquisition of land by foreigners.	
II. SECTOR-SPECIFIC COMMITMENTS			
4. DISTRIBUTION SERVICES C. Retailing services (CPC 631, 632)	(1) Unbound (except for mail order: none).	(1) Unbound (except for mail order: none).	
	(2) None.	(2) None.	
	(3) Foreign equity participation limited to 51 per cent.	(3) Investment grants are available only to companies controlled by Arcadian nationals.	
	(4) Unbound, except as indicated in horizontal section.	(4) Unbound.	

Figure 3

is further clarified by reference to the United Nations provisional Central Product Classification (CPC), commitments vary widely across modes. Most liberal are those for mode 2 (consumption abroad), where Arcadia is bound not to take any measure under either Article XVI or XVII that would prevent or discourage its residents from shopping abroad.

Entries in schedules should remain confined to measures incompatible with either the market access or national treatment provisions of the GATS and to any additional commitments a Member may want to undertake under Article XVIII. Schedules would not provide legal cover for measures inconsistent with other provisions of the Agreement, including the MFN requirement under Article II or the obligation under Article VI:1 to reasonable, objective and impartial administration of measures of general application. MFN-inconsistent measures that have not been included in the relevant list need to be rescinded, and the same applies to any measures inconsistent with Article VI. The trade-impeding effects associated with non-discriminatory domestic regulation – qualification requirements for teachers, lawyers or accountants; minimum capital requirements for banks; mandatory liability insurance for doctors and so on – do not call for scheduling per se. As noted before, the Agreement clearly distinguishes between, on the one hand, trade liberalization under specific commitments and, on the other hand, domestic regulation for quality and other legitimate policy purposes. By the same token, there is no need to schedule access restrictions such as sales bans on arms or pornographic material and the like that fall under the general exceptions of Article XIV or prudential measures aimed to ensure the stability and integrity of the financial services sector.

3

A CLOSER LOOK AT DOMESTIC REGULATION

PURPOSE AND EFFECTS OF REGULATION

As noted before, the GATS makes a clear distinction between domestic regulation and measures subject to trade liberalization. On the one hand, it explicitly recognizes the continued right (and, possibly, the need) of Members to enforce domestic policy objectives through regulation. On the other hand, it promotes the objective of progressive liberalization, consisting of expanding and/or improving existing commitments on market access and national treatment.

Effective regulation – or re-regulation – can be a precondition for liberalization to produce the expected efficiency gains without compromising on quality and other policy objectives. For example, the opening of a hitherto restricted market may need to be accompanied by the introduction of new licensing mechanisms and public service obligations for quality and social policy reasons. Since many services contracts involve customized, not yet existing products (medical intervention, legal advice, etc.), the need for regulatory protection is particularly evident.

By the same token, however, it may be necessary to ensure that the benefits from liberalization are not frustrated by ineffective or inconsistent regulation. Many regulatory regimes have evolved in response to immediate problems and challenges, without much thought being given to trade and efficiency considerations. Moreover, regulatory responsibilities tend to be spread across ministries and agencies (Finance, Justice, Construction, Transport, Health, Education, etc.) and levels of government without much communication, let alone co-ordination.

Examples of public policy objectives that might require regulatory support:

> equitable access, regardless of income or location, to a given service;
> consumer protection (including through information and control);
> job creation in disadvantaged regions;
> labour market integration of disadvantaged persons;
> reduction of environmental impacts and other externalities;
> macroeconomic stability;
> avoidance of market dominance and anti-competitive conduct;
> avoidance of tax evasion, fraud and so on

Governments remain free under the GATS to pursue such policy objectives even in sectors where they have undertaken full commitments on market access and national treatment.

Food for thought

Could you give examples of sectors where the above policy objectives are relevant? What measures might be used?

Possible reply

Equitable access

Sectors: transport; education; health; telecommunication services

Measures: cross-subsidization and other financial incentives; universal service obligation as licensing condition

Consumer protection

Sectors: professional services; financial services; health services

Policies: prudential and other technical standards; publication requirements; qualification requirements for professionals; licensing/certification of facilities

Job creation in disadvantaged regions

Sectors: infrastructural services such as railways or maritime transport; long-term health care (rehabilitation centres, etc.)

Policies: twinning requirements relating activities in urban centres to those in remote areas (repair shops, shipyards, health facilities, etc.)

Integration of disadvantaged persons

Sectors: potentially all service suppliers beyond a certain minimum size

Policies: obligation to employ a certain percentage of handicapped persons

Reduction of environmental impacts and other externalities

Sectors: road transport; tourism

Policies: prohibition of weekend or night traffic; zoning laws; environment-related standards

Macroeconomic stability

Sectors: financial services

Policies: minimum equity requirements; diversification of assets; other prudential standards

Avoidance of market dominance and anti-competitive conduct

Sectors: potentially all sectors prone to market concentration (including sectors with strong network effects and interconnection needs (transport, telecom) and previous monopoly areas)

Policies: prohibition of collusive arrangements; monitoring of market developments; price surveillance; harmonization of technical standards; promotion of new market entries

Avoidance of tax evasion, fraud, etc.

Sectors: all

Policies: disclosure requirements; monitoring and policing

DISCIPLINES FOR DOMESTIC REGULATION

Regulations that are not intended to serve protective purposes under Articles XVI and XVII may nevertheless severely restrict trade. Such restrictive effects may be justified in view of a prevailing policy objective, or they may be due to excessive and/or inefficient intervention. The latter possibility seems to be stronger in services than in merchandise trade, given the defining role of regulation for products that are intangible by nature and the intrinsically close relationship between product and supplier.

Because of the importance of the domestic regulatory environment as a context for trade, the Council for Trade in Services has been given a particular negotiating mandate in Article VI:4. It allows the Council to develop, in appropriate bodies, any necessary disciplines to prevent domestic regulations (qualification requirements and procedures, technical standards and licensing requirements) from constituting unnecessary barriers to trade. The Working Party on Domestic Regulation (WPDR) has been established for that purpose.

The disciplines envisaged under Article VI:4 are intended to ensure that domestic regulations are, *inter alia*,

(a) based on objective and transparent criteria, such as competence and the ability to supply the service;
(b) not more burdensome than necessary to ensure the quality of the service;
(c) in the case of licensing procedures, not in themselves a restriction on the supply of the service.

While it is difficult to predict the outcome of current work, there is already some sort of precedent which may provide guidance: The Disciplines on Domestic Regulation in the Accountancy Sector (document S/L/64), approved by the Services Council in December 1998. The relevant Council Decision (document S/L/63) provides that the "accountancy disciplines" are applicable only to Members who have scheduled specific commitments on accountancy. The disciplines are to be integrated into the GATS, together with any new results the WPDR may achieve in the interim, at the end of the current round. A core feature of the disciplines is their focus on (non-discriminatory) regulations that are not subject to scheduling under Articles XVI and XVII.

Measures relating to licensing, qualifications and technical standards which discriminate between foreign and domestic suppliers, whether formally or in fact, would need to be scheduled as national treatment limitation in the sectors where GATS commitments have been made.

Pending the entry into force of the disciplines under Article VI:4, Members are required not to apply their domestic regulation in a way that would nullify or impair specific commitments or be incompatible with the three above criteria, or in a way that could not have reasonably been expected at the time when the relevant commitments were made.

POTENTIALLY RELEVANT PRINCIPLES

The WPDR has been reviewing principles that could form a framework for regulatory development.

(a) Necessity
Domestic regulations should not be more trade restrictive or burdensome than necessary to achieve a specific, legitimate objective. Without a clear statement of purpose, it would be difficult to measure the effectiveness of a regulation after implementation.

(b) Transparency
Information on regulatory principles and process should be accessible to all parties concerned. Relevant criteria include:
reasonable advance notice before implementation;
public availability to service suppliers – easy to find, easy to read;
specification of reasonable time periods for responding to applications;
information provided as to why an application was declined; and
information provided on procedures for review of administrative decisions.

(c) Equivalence
Account should be taken of the relevant qualifications and experience that a supplier may have obtained abroad.

(d) International standards
Acceptance of international standards could facilitate the evaluation of qualifications obtained abroad.

Other principles that have been raised for discussion include impartial application; proportionality (any penalties for non-performance should bear a reasonable relationship to the risks involved); a regular review process; minimization of the administrative burden involved; and objective criteria linked to international standards.

DEVELOPING NEW REGULATIONS –
HOW TO PROCEED

In the process of regulatory review and development, the ministries and agencies involved may need to address four categories of issues.

1. The purpose of the regulation
   The national policy objective and the requirement for new regulation should be clear.
2. How to ensure effectiveness
   Check the principles listed in the previous section.
3. Criteria for implementation and administration
   Transparent and impartial procedures;
   timely information for applicants on status of processing;
   proper training and supervision of officials involved;
   permanent monitoring for compliance with underlying objectives.
4. Recourse possibilities for adversely affected suppliers
   The relevant process should be clearly delineated, reasonably timely and not unduly burdensome.

One of the barriers to trade expansion for service suppliers is multiple licensing and certification requirements in export markets. Such requirements may not only prove costly from the suppliers' perspective, but could unnecessarily restrict competition – and thus have unwarranted price effects – for potential users. To help solve such problems, Members have concluded mutual recognition agreements (MRAs) in appropriate cases or have autonomously recognized education and training obtained in other jurisdictions. While potentially in conflict with the MFN obligation under Article II, GATS Article VII allows for such measures as long as there are adequate provisions for other Members to negotiate accession and/or achieve recognition of their requirements and certificates, and the measures do not constitute a means of discrimination or a disguised restriction on trade.

4

HOW THE GATS IS ADMINISTERED

COUNCIL FOR TRADE IN SERVICES

The top decision-making body of the WTO is the Ministerial Conference, which is composed of representatives of all Members and meets every two years. In the interim, the Conference is represented by the General Council. The Council for Trade in Services operates under the guidance of the General Council and is responsible for overseeing the functioning of the GATS. It is open to all WTO Members and meets several times a year in regular session and, for the conduct of the ongoing services negotiations, in special session. Minutes of meetings can be found on the WTO website.

SUBSIDIARY BODIES

The Council for Trade in Services has instituted four subsidiary bodies to deal with individual sectors or technical issues and/or to conduct negotiations in rule-making areas not finally concluded during the Uruguay Round.

The *Committee on Trade in Financial Services* discusses trade and regulatory developments in financial services and reviews the application of the GATS to this sector. As part of its monitoring function, the Committee receives periodic updates from the few Members that have not yet ratified the Fifth Protocol. (The Protocol is intended to ensure implementation of the results of the negotiations on financial services which were extended, among some seventy Members, until December 1997.)

The *Working Party on Domestic Regulation* is mandated, pursuant to Article VI:4, to develop disciplines in the area of domestic regulation. The Working Party was set up in April 1999 to replace, equipped with a broader mandate, the Working Party on Professional Services. In May 1997 the latter had passed (voluntary) Guidelines for Mutual Recognition Agreements or Arrangements in the Accountancy Sector (S/WPPS/W/12) and, in December 1998, the Council for Trade in Services adopted the Disciplines on Domestic Regulation in the Accountancy Sector (S/L/64). The Accountancy Disciplines currently apply on a best-endeavours basis; in the context of the current services round they are to be formally integrated into the GATS.

The *Working Party on GATS Rules* has three negotiating mandates: Emergency Safeguard Measures (Article X), Government Procurement (Article XIII) and

Subsidies (Article XV (see further Chapter 6)). Of these, only the negotiations on emergency safeguards were initially subject to a deadline specified in the Agreement; it has since been extended repeatedly and finally been replaced by an open-ended Council Decision. The Guidelines and Procedures for the Services Negotiations (S/L/93) provide that Members "shall aim to complete" the negotiations in the two other areas (government procurement and subsidies) and those under Article VI:4 prior to the conclusion of the negotiations on specific commitments in the new round.

In March 2001 the *Committee on Specific Commitments* concluded its revision of the Guidelines for the Scheduling of Specific Commitments, which were subsequently adopted by the Council for Trade in Services (S/L/92). The Guidelines, initially developed at an advanced stage of the Uruguay Round, are intended to provide technical advice for the scheduling of commitments and thus enhance the comparability and consistency of schedules; they are a non-binding document. Further, the Committee has discussed classification issues – with a focus on legal services, postal and courier services, the construction industry, environmental services and energy services – and other, predominantly technical, matters relating to the scheduling of commitments and the completion of schedules at the end of the current negotiations.

ROLE OF THE WTO SECRETARIAT

The WTO Secretariat assists Members in the development, administration and application of the various agreements. This entails a variety of supporting functions for relevant WTO bodies (councils, committees, working parties, etc.), the provision of technical assistance and advice to developing countries and countries in accession, the analyses of trade and trade policy developments in individual economies and overall, and the contribution of legal information and advice in dispute cases. The Secretariat is headed by a Director General and has some 500 staff, including some 150 professionals in operational divisions (excluding interpretation, translation, etc.). Work related to the GATS is provided and/or co-ordinated by the Trade in Services Division. The International Trade Centre UNCTAD/WTO, also with headquarters in Geneva, provides trade-related intelligence and expertise for economic operators (exporters, importers and their associations).

DISPUTE SETTLEMENT PROCEDURES

Effective dispute resolution – from the stage of friction to consultation, complaint, adjudication and implementation – is critical to the effective functioning of the WTO Agreements. In the event of problems related to the operation of the GATS, Articles XXII and XXIII provide the framework for consultations and, if need be,

Table 1. *Timeframes for dispute settlement stages.*

Stage	Timeframe
Consultations, mediation, etc	60 days
Panel set up and panellists appointed	45 days
Final panel report to parties	6 months
Final panel report to WTO Members	3 weeks
Dispute Settlement Body adopts report	60 days
Total (without appeal)	**12 months**
Appellate Body report	90 days
Dispute Settlement Body adopts Appellate Body report	30 days
Total (with appeal)	**16 months**

DISPUTE SETTLEMENT WITHIN THE WTO

Step 1: A Member requests consultations with another Member which it considers to have breached its obligations or to have otherwise impaired benefits under the GATS.

Step 2: Consultations between the two Members are held with the aim of reaching a mutually satisfactory solution.

Step 3: If the consultations fail to resolve the issue, the complaining Member may request the establishment of a panel of three independent experts. These are generally chosen from an existing roster of qualified panellists.

Step 4: The panel examines the complaint in the light of the relevant legal obligations, and has six months in which to issue a report with binding recommendations for adoption by the dispute settlement body (DSB).

Step 5: Any party to the dispute may appeal the panel ruling before the WTO Appellate Body.

Step 6: The Appellate Body examines the appeal, and has up to ninety days to deliver its report.

Step 7: The panel ruling is adopted by the DSB (including any modifications decided by the Appellate Body), unless there is consensus not to adopt.

Step 8: The Member concerned is given time for implementation.

Step 9: In the absence of full implementation within the specified period, a party to the dispute may request permission from the DSB to suspend equivalent commitments with respect to this Member.

Figure 4

dispute settlement and enforcement among Members. The relevant provisions of the Dispute Settlement Understanding (DSU) apply.

The preferred outcome of the DSU process is resolution through consultation, rather than through panel rulings. If these are nevertheless needed, an initial ruling by an independent panel is endorsed (unless there is a full consensus that it be rejected) by the WTO's General Council which in this case meets as the Dispute Settlement Body. Appeals based on points of law are possible. Figure 4 outlines the dispute settlement process.

The DSU provides a timeframe for each of the dispute settlement stages (see Table 1). If a case runs its full course to a first ruling, it should not normally take more than one year, or 16 months if the case is appealed. The agreed time limits are flexible and, if the case is considered to be urgent, it could take as little as nine months. Since a ruling is automatically adopted unless there is a consensus to reject it, any dissatisfied Member would need to persuade all other WTO Members (including all parties to the case) of its view.

The DSB has the sole authority to establish panels to consider the case, and to accept or reject the findings. If the respondent Member loses, it must abide by the panel's or the Appellate Body's recommendations and state its intention to do so at a DSB meeting held within thirty days of the report's adoption. If immediate compliance proves impractical, the Member will be afforded a "reasonable period of time".

If the Member feels unable to act in time, it has to enter into negotiations with the complaining Member(s) in order to agree on mutually acceptable compensation. If this proves impossible within twenty days, the complaining Member may ask the DSB for permission to impose limited trade sanctions ("suspend concessions or obligations") against the other Member. The DSB is to grant authorization unless there is a consensus against this request.

In principle, sanctions should be imposed within the sector concerned. If this is not practical or not effective, a different sector under the same agreement may be chosen. As a last resort, action may be taken under another agreement. The objective is to minimize the risk of unrelated sectors and legal frameworks being drawn into the matter while at the same time ensuring effectiveness.

5

THE ROLE AND RESPONSIBILITIES OF MEMBER GOVERNMENTS

THE MINISTRIES AND AGENCIES INVOLVED

The GATS is a relatively new agreement. National administrations thus have less experience in dealing with GATS-related issues than with "traditional" trade problems under the GATT, and they do not normally have a central structure for co-ordinating their services-related policies. A wide range of ministries and agencies at various government levels may be involved.

Regulation of services often occurs in fact at sub-federal levels (state/province/municipality or parish) or, in some instances (e.g., professional licensing), has been delegated to private-sector organizations. A related challenge is the fact that there are some 160 service sub-sectors involved, which would be difficult for any central agency to oversee. In order to ensure compliance with existing obligations, and to participate effectively in the new round, national administrations may find it useful to create sector- or issue-related working groups. Table 2 suggests how such groups might be composed.

Given the regulatory intensity of many service activities and the range of sectors involved, proper co-ordination and information across agencies and government levels is critical for at least three purposes:

(i) ensuring awareness of the types of GATS-related measures falling under a ministry's or agency's jurisdiction;

(ii) ensuring that each ministry/agency has properly identified and analyzed – against the background of existing GATS obligations, including specific commitments – its current use of measures; and

(iii) ensuring that, in preparing new measures, relevant GATS obligations – including notification requirements – are taken into account and complied with.

As noted before, apart from specific commitments, there are in principle two types of legal obligations under the Agreement: unconditional obligations that apply across all services covered by the GATS, and conditional obligations that apply only to sectors where specific commitments have been made.

(a) Obligations in all sectors falling under the GATS ("unconditional"):
to ensure compliance with the MFN requirement (Article II);
to publish all measures pertaining to or affecting the operation of GATS (Article III:1);

Table 2. *Possible composition of the government working groups*

Government working group	Government working group composition	
	Responsible government ministries/agencies	Other potentially relevant bodies
Business services	Industry and Commerce Agriculture Fisheries Forestry Mining Justice	Real Estate Board Professional Licensing Registrar National Research Council
Communication services	Communications Industry and Commerce Culture and Education	Telecom Regulator Postal Service Provider National Film Board National News Service
Construction and related engineering services	Public Works Industry and Commerce	Housing Authority Planning and Zoning Authority
Distribution services	Industry and Commerce Customs Authority	Planning and Zoning Authority
Educational services	Culture and Education Industry and Commerce	
Environmental services	Environment Industry and Commerce	Waste Disposal Authority Recycling Authority
Financial services	Finance Central Bank Insurance/Banking Registrar Securities Regulator Pension Fund Regulator	
Health-related and social services	Health Social Welfare Women and Families	Natural Disaster Agency Infectious Disease Authority Vocational Rehabilitation
Recreational, cultural and sporting services	Culture and Education Sports Parks Authority	National Museum National Library National Arts Council National Film Agency
Tourism and travel-related services	Tourism Parks Authority	Planning and Zoning Authority
Transport services	Transportation Vehicle Licensing	Port Authority Airport Authority Rail operators
Other services	Utilities Regulator	Public utilities (water, gas, electricity)

(cont.)

Table 2. (*cont.*)

| Government working group | Government working group composition | |
	Responsible government ministries/agencies	Other potentially relevant bodies
Cross-sector: modes of supply and e-trade	Immigration Authority Investment Authority Export Development Authority Company Registry Land Title Registry Industry and Commerce	
Cross-sector: standards and professional credentials	Standards Agency Employment Standards Worker's Compensation Board Licensing and Work Permits Ministry of Trade	Professional services associations
Cross-sector: co-ordination among levels of government	Industry and Commerce	
Cross-sector: economic and labour force development	Human Resource Development Human Rights Commission Micro-Enterprises Taxation Authority Planning and Zoning Authority Ministry of Labour	

Source: Adapted from OECD, 2002.

> to institute legal complaints mechanisms for affected suppliers (Article VI:2);
> to ensure that recognition measures are compatible with the provisions of Article VII;
> to prevent monopolies from undermining the MFN requirement (Article VIII:1); and
> to consult with other Members, upon request, on business practices that may restrain competition (Article IX:2).

(b) Obligations in sectors in which GATS commitments have been undertaken ("conditional"):

> to notify any new laws, regulations etc. that significantly affect trade (Article III:3);

to administer regulations in a reasonable, objective and impartial manner (Article VI:1);

to prevent licensing and qualification requirements and technical standards from nullifying or impairing commitments (relevant criteria are specified in Article VI:5);

to prevent monopolies from undermining commitments (Article VIII:1 and 2); and

to ensure the absence of restrictions on payments and transfers (Article XI:1)

NOTIFICATIONS

In addition to their transparency obligations under Article (III:1) and 3 (see above), Members have further notification and information requirements in specified circumstances. In particular, they need to notify and/or provide information on

the establishment of enquiry points pursuant to Article (III:4) and of contact points pursuant to Article IV:2 (document S/L/23);

the conclusion, enlargement or significant modification of economic integration agreements (Article V:7a);

the progress on implementation if such agreements are phased in (Article V:7b);

the intention to "withdraw or modify a specific commitment" in the context of an economic integration agreement (Article V:5);

labour markets integration agreements (Article V *bis*);

existing recognition measures (within twelve months of the GATS taking effect) and whether these are based on mutual agreement (Article VII:4a);

the opening of negotiations on a mutual recognition agreement (Article VII:4b);

the adoption or significant modification of recognition measures (Article VII:4c);

intentions to grant monopoly rights or exclusive service supplier status in services covered by specific commitments (Article VIII:4);

trade restrictions adopted or maintained due to serious balance-of-payments or external financial difficulties or threat thereof (Article XII:4);

the invocation of security exceptions pursuant to Article XIV *bis* (information to be provided "to the fullest extent possible");

the intention to modify or withdraw a scheduled commitment (Articles XXI:1b and X:2); and

the introduction of an MFN-consistent regime at the termination of the relevant exemption (para. 7 of the Annex on Article II Exemptions).

ENQUIRY POINTS

Given the crucial role of regulation in determining market entry and market participation in many services sectors, there are various provisions in the Agreement to improve the transparency of Members' regulatory regimes. Apart from various notification and information requirements, these include the obligation on all Members to maintain one or more enquiry points. At such points, other Members can request and receive specific information on measures of general application or international agreements affecting services trade (Article III:4). A list of these enquiry points is available on the WTO website (www.wto.org).

Enquiry points are intended only for government access. Queries from the business community may be channelled through the home-country government to the enquiry point of the Member concerned. In order for these points to be effective, they must have at their disposal an inventory or a database of relevant measures and international agreements within the meaning of Article III:1 and 3. Increasingly, such information is being made more generally available through searchable websites.

CONTACT POINTS

To help to increase the participation of developing countries in trade, developed country Members – and, to the extent possible, other Members – are required to establish contact points. These are intended to facilitate the access of developing countries' service suppliers to information regarding "commercial and technical aspects of the supply of services; registration, recognition and obtaining of professional qualifications; and the availability of services technology" (Article IV:2).

6

THE CHALLENGES AHEAD

THE DOHA DEVELOPMENT AGENDA

The Uruguay Round marked only a first step in a longer-term process of services liberalization within a multilateral framework. The importance of the Round lay less in its improving actual market conditions than in creating a completely new system of rules and disciplines for future trade liberalization. This may also explain why the GATS, in Article XIX:1, already provides for a new round of services negotiations to start not later than five years from the date of entry into force of the Agreement.

Consequently a new services round was launched in January 2000. It aims to achieve a progressively higher level of liberalization of services trade while "promoting the interests of all participants on a mutually advantageous basis and . . . securing an overall balance of rights and obligations" (Article XIX:1). Although the Seattle Ministerial Conference in late November 1999 failed to agree on launching a larger trade round, the mandate to negotiate on services was never put in doubt. In contrast to the preparatory stages of the Uruguay Round, Members no longer focused on whether, but rather on how, to promote services liberalization within the multilateral system.

As a first step in 2000, and as part of an information exchange programme mandated at the Singapore Ministerial Conference, the WTO Secretariat prepared a series of background papers on major services sectors (available on the WTO website) to stimulate policy discussion and promote dissemination of relevant information among Members. In March 2001 the Council for Trade in Services adopted Guidelines and Procedures for the services negotiations (document S/L/93) as provided for in Article XIX:3. Major elements include a reaffirmation of the right to regulate and to introduce new regulations on the supply of services; the objective of increasing participation by developing countries in services trade; and the preservation of the existing structure and principles of the GATS, including listing the sectors in which commitments are made and the four modes of supply. Certain new elements have been added, such as the explicit recognition of the needs of small and medium-sized service suppliers; a reference to the request–offer approach as the main method of negotiation; and the continuation of the assessment of trade in services, mandated under Article XIX:3, as an ongoing activity of the Council for Trade in Services.

The Negotiating Guidelines further provide that the rule-making negotiations inherited from the Uruguay Round ("built-in agenda") in the areas of subsidies, government procurement and domestic regulation be concluded prior to the completion of the negotiations on specific commitments (Article IV:2). The negotiations on safeguards under Article X were made subject to an earlier deadline (15 March 2002), which has since been revised. A Decision by the Council for Trade in Services of March 2004 now provides that, subject to the outcome of the negotiating mandate in Article X:1, the results shall enter into force not later than the results of the current round of services negotiations.

In November 2001 the Ministerial Conference in Doha agreed on a comprehensive negotiating agenda which is to be concluded by 1 January 2005. The various negotiating mandates – on agriculture, services, "traditional" market access issues, WTO rules, trade and environment and so on – form part of a "single undertaking" (para. 47). It is implemented under the authority of a Trade Negotiations Committee (TNC) which reports to the General Council.

The Ministerial Declaration confirms the Services Negotiating Guidelines of March 2001 and places them in the overall timeframe of the Doha Development Agenda. Initial requests for new or improved services commitments were to be submitted by 30 June 2002, with initial offers being due by 31 March 2003.

The importance for services of the Declaration goes, however, beyond its embracing the Negotiating Guidelines of 2001. This is for at least two reasons. First, the success of the Doha Conference and its integration of services into a wider negotiating context testifies to the resilience of the multilateral framework and provides an important political boost. Second, the Declaration provides for negotiations in areas beyond those addressed in the Guidelines. Cases in point are a mandate to negotiate the removal or reduction of trade barriers on environmental goods and services, and a commitment to commence negotiations, after the Fifth Ministerial Conference (held in Cancún, Mexico, in September 2003), on the interaction between trade and competition policy and on transparency in government procurement. The work programme on electronic commerce, launched by the Geneva Ministerial Conference in 1998, is to continue under the aegis of the General Council.

THE MANDATED REVIEW OF MFN EXEMPTIONS

Most-favoured-nation treatment is a fundamental principle of the multilateral trading system as it was conceived after World War II and reconfigured in the Uruguay Round (see Chapter 1). Any departures should thus be limited to exceptional circumstances and, where possible, be phased out over time.

The Annex on Article II Exemptions stipulates that MFN exemptions should not exceed in principle ten years, and provides for a review of all existing measures that had been granted for periods of more than five years. The latter review is destined to examine whether the conditions that led to the creation of the exemptions still prevail. More importantly, the Annex on Article II Exemptions also requires that MFN exemptions be subject to negotiation in any subsequent trade round.

The first review was concluded in May 2001; Members decided to conduct another review not later than June 2004.

NEGOTIATIONS ON GATS RULES

The GATS contains several negotiating mandates in rule-making areas which Members felt unable to consider in detail within the timeframe of the Uruguay Round. These negotiations are conducted by two working parties, one on Domestic Regulation (see "Disciplines for domestic regulation" in Chapter 3 and "Subsidiary bodies" in Chapter 4) and one on GATS Rules. The latter working party is charged with negotiations on emergency safeguards (Article X), government procurement (Article XIII), and subsidies (Article XV).

Emergency safeguards

Emergency safeguards in services may be expected to allow for the temporary suspension of market access, national treatment and/or any additional commitments that Members may have assumed in individual sectors. Any such mechanism, should it be agreed to by Members, would need to be based on the principle of non-discrimination. It would complement existing provisions under the GATS that already allow for temporary or permanent departures from general obligations or specific commitments. Relevant provisions include Article XII if a Member experiences serious balance of payments and external financial difficulties; Article XIV if action is deemed necessary for overriding policy concerns such as protection of life and health or protection of public morals; and Article XXI if a Member intends to withdraw or modify a commitment on a permanent basis.

In contrasting to these provisions, a safeguards clause might be used to ease adjustment pressures in situations where a particular industry is threatened by a sudden increase in foreign supplies. If the Safeguards Agreement for goods is used as a precedent, the onus would be on a protection-seeking industry to demonstrate that a causal link exists between such increases in supplies and its suffering serious injury.

There are two main schools of thought among Members. One group is not convinced that such a mechanism is desirable, given the scheduling flexibility under the GATS and the risk of undermining the stability of existing commitments through new emergency provisions. There are also doubts whether a services safeguard would be workable in practice. Sceptical Members point to the scarcity of reliable trade and production data in many sectors, and the technical complexities associated with the multi-modal structure of the GATS. Another group of Members feels that the availability of safeguards in the event of unforeseeable market disruptions would encourage more liberal commitments in services negotiations. In their view, abuse could be avoided through strict procedural disciplines. Data problems should not be exaggerated, given the existence in many sectors of professional associations, regulators and licensing bodies that compile relevant information.

GOVERNMENT PROCUREMENT

The share of government purchases of services – from postal and communication services to transport and financial services – is significant in many markets, and so are the trade effects that may result from access restrictions. The GATS imposes no effective disciplines, however, on governments' use of such restrictions, whether in the form of exclusions of foreign participation, or of preferential margins favouring domestic suppliers.

Article XIII provides that the MFN obligation (Article II) and any existing commitments on market access and national treatment (Articles XVI and XVII) do not apply to the procurement of services for governmental purposes. It is for the individual Members to balance the fiscal cost and structural inefficiencies that may be associated with purchasing restrictions and/or preferences with their expected contribution to employment, development and other policy objectives. However, Article XIII provides for negotiations to be conducted under the GATS. Although these negotiations started relatively soon after the Uruguay Round, together with those in the other rule-making areas, progress has been limited to date. It remains to be seen whether the new round will give a boost.

The only current procurement disciplines under WTO provisions are those contained in the Plurilateral Agreement on Government Procurement, whose scope is confined to a limited number of mostly economically advanced Members. The Agreement applies to purchases of goods and services and provides for transparency and, in specifically listed sectors, non-discrimination in the award process among signatories. Further, the Doha Declaration foresees negotiations after the Fifth Ministerial Conference on transparency in government procurement.

SUBSIDIES

Like other measures affecting trade in services, subsidies are already subject to the GATS. The unconditional general obligations, including MFN treatment, thus apply. In scheduled sectors, these are complemented by the national treatment obligation, subject to any limitations that may have been inscribed, and a variety of conditional obligations.

Article XV nevertheless provides for negotiations on disciplines that may be necessary to avoid trade-distortive effects. The appropriateness of countervailing measures shall also be addressed. While the Agreement provides no further guidance, it may be assumed that the negotiating mandate covers trade distortions associated with subsidies in areas beyond the modal definition of GATS (e.g. cross-border exports) or in sectors or modes not covered by specific commitments in the relevant Member's schedule.

The WTO Agreement on Subsidies and Countervailing Measures was developed for trade in goods, and it may not necessarily prove an appropriate model for services. Governments may want to retain broader scope for subsidising in pursuit of social, cultural and general development objectives. While Article XV:1

of the GATS also provides for an information exchange on subsidies among Members, very little information has been provided to date. This may reflect a certain lack of negotiating interest, but might also be attributed to definitional and data problems.

THE ASSESSMENT OF TRADE IN SERVICES

Article XIX:3 provides that prior to establishing the negotiating guidelines for a new round, "the Council for Trade in Services shall carry out an assessment of trade in services in overall terms and on a sectoral basis with reference to the objectives of this Agreement, including those set out in paragraph 1 of Article IV". While discussed at virtually all meetings of the Services Council since 1998–99, delegations have found it difficult to arrive at a common assessment. This may be due not only to natural divergences in policy objectives and negotiating interest, but also to problems of data availability and comparability across countries, sectors and modes. The commitments contained in schedules can hardly be considered to be meaningful reference points for an assessment, given that they cover only a limited number of sectors and that most entries remained confined to locking in status quo conditions in the early 1990s. In many cases they have since been overtaken by autonomous policy reforms.

At the request of the Council for Trade in Services, the WTO Secretariat prepared numerous background papers in 1998 and 1999, mostly available on the WTO website, with potentially relevant information. A Secretariat Note of late 2001 (document S/CSS/W/117) discusses conceivable criteria for Members' own assessment of services performance. Ideally, deliberations in the Services Council would be based on such national assessments. To advance the process further, the Council for Trade in Services held a Symposium on Assessment of Trade in Services in early 2002; it offered academic researchers and representatives of national and international institutions a forum in which to present and discuss relevant findings. Most presentations are available on the WTO website.

WORK PROGRAMME ON E-COMMERCE

A fundamental structural change affecting services trade is the proliferation of Internet use, with the number of users said to be doubling every year. Compared with some 4.5 million in 1991, there were over 500 million users by the end of 2000. Encryption technologies to address data security concerns have advanced sufficiently for online sales to accelerate.

The rapid changes in information technology (IT) and telecommunications have resulted in a virtually borderless global economy allowing any service that can be digitized and transmitted electronically to be produced and delivered anywhere in the world. Electronic commerce may thus prove a "great equalizer" that helps to reduce, even eliminate, distance-related barriers to trade, but it can also exacerbate a so-called "digital divide" vis-à-vis countries with infrastructural deficiencies. For regions presently without Internet access, going online can make the difference between international market integration or increasing marginalization.

The Internet provides a low-cost, highly efficient way to approach potential customers world-wide. It will have multiple influences on trade flows and, possibly, trade negotiations. One of the biggest challenges is creating a regulatory environment for e-business and e-trade that is responsive to the rapid changes in technology. E-governance initiatives and comprehensive IT development strategies can help to build familiarity among policy makers and trade negotiators.

The Doha Declaration has continued the moratorium on imposing customs duties on electronic transmissions (document WT/MIN(01)/DEC/1, para.34). Debate continues on whether some products which can be delivered both on a physical carrier and in purely electronic form (e.g., computer software) should best be classified as services or goods. The classification of such transactions determines whether GATT or GATS applies, with potentially important implications for WTO Members' legal obligations in the areas concerned.

The second WTO Ministerial Conference in 1998 adopted a Declaration on Global Electronic Commerce "to establish a comprehensive work programme to examine all trade-related issues relating to global electronic commerce, taking into account the economic, financial, and development needs of developing countries". Discussions in relation to GATS have focused on the idea of maintaining the integrity of the GATS definition of trade in services (Article I:2), which does not rule out any technological means by which the services may be supplied.

GATS provisions may be relevant, at least indirectly, to many concerns surrounding the formulation of e-commerce or Internet law and policy. For example, the general exceptions (Article XIV) may actually govern most measures designed to deal with online privacy protection, illegal or illicit content, cybercrime and fraud, enforcement of contracts, consumer protection and taxation. Governments may even resort to measures that are otherwise inconsistent with GATS obligations – bearing in mind that disciplines on the use of the exception are built into the provision itself. Specifically, such measures must be "necessary" to meet the objective concerned (i.e. the stated objective cannot effectively be met without resort to inconsistent measures), they may not discriminate unjustifiably against particular countries and they may not be used as disguised trade restrictions (i.e. used as a back-door means to protect markets).

The role of the WTO, and GATS, will be to ensure that the broad economic advantages of multilateral rules and obligations will accrue to electronic supplies, just as they do to other forms of trade. Judging by some of the negotiating proposals (e.g. on telecom and computer services) submitted thus far by both developed and developing country Members, there is a widely held view that GATS bindings can be used to strengthen countries' capacity to take advantage of e-commerce and narrow the digital divide. In addition to telecom and computer services, financial payments services, advertising services and delivery services have also been mentioned as components of an e-commerce enabling "infrastructure". Various professional services and IT services, "back-office" services in particular, as well as education and health services, are among the potential beneficiaries in developing countries of improved e-commerce and Internet capacity. Fora other than the WTO may be equipped to deal with technical issues such as authentication, encryption, Internet governance and domain names or cultural and human resource issues such as the encouragement of diversity in local and linguistic content, computer literacy and education.

The current state of play under the GATS discussions is still best summed up by a progress report produced by the GATS Council in 1999 (document S/C/W/8). It stated that "while discussion will continue on all of the issues so far considered, Members agreed that some issues would require substantial further study before their implications could be properly understood". On some other issues, however, discussions had progressed more closely towards reaching a common understanding:

> The electronic delivery of services falls within the scope of the GATS, since the Agreement applies to all services regardless of the means by which they are delivered, and electronic delivery can take place under any of the four modes of supply. Measures affecting the electronic delivery of services are measures affecting trade in services and would therefore be covered by GATS obligations.
>
> The technological neutrality of the Agreement would also mean that the electronic supply of services is permitted by specific commitments unless the schedule states otherwise.
>
> All GATS provisions, whether relating to general obligations (e.g. MFN, transparency, domestic regulation, competition, payments and transfer, etc.) or specific commitments (market access, national treatment or additional commitments), are applicable to the supply of services through electronic means.

The same report identified issues requiring further examination. The focus is on clarifying the application of current GATS provisions in the light of developments on the Internet and in e-trade in services. Examples are:

> Clarification of the distinction between mode 1 (cross-border) and mode 2 (consumption abroad) in situations where a service is being delivered electronically.
>
> Classification and scheduling of new services that might arise in the context of electronic commerce, and clarifying the classification and improving the scheduling of Internet access and related services.
>
> Further work on the implications of Article VI for domestic regulations affecting electronic commerce.
>
> Clarification of the scope of the Annex on Telecommunications in relation to access to and use of Internet access and other related services and

the applicability of the principles contained in the Reference Paper on basic telecommunications to electronic commerce and whether there is a need to develop any additional disciplines under the GATS.

Further study of the application of customs duties on electronic transmissions and, correspondingly, the possible implications of maintaining the moratorium on such duties.

In spite of the recognized need for further examination of some details related to GATS coverage and treatment of e-commerce, the services negotiations are proceeding apace. Moreover, they appear to be proceeding under an implicit assumption that e-commerce is an integral part of what is being covered by rule-making and access negotiations, rather than a separate item.

7

PREPARING REQUESTS AND OFFERS

NEGOTIATING APPROACHES

In their Uruguay Round schedules many Members confined commitments to binding status quo conditions in a limited range of sectors. The number of services included, and the levels of access bound, in general remained modest. This may have been due to a variety of factors: the preference of governments to play it safe, that is to avoid tensions over the interpretation and application of a completely new set of rules; reticence on the part of services-related ministries and agencies which had no prior experience of international trade negotiations; the difficulties of small administrations, short of resources, to keep pace with the negotiating process in Geneva; and the instincts of seasoned negotiators, who, in the absence of requests from large trading partners, may have preferred to keep silent.

In order to benefit from GATS negotiations, however, it is necessary for governments to reconsider old habits. As noted above, unlike traditional trade agreements for goods, the GATS extends to consumer movements (mode 2) and the movement of production factors – in the form of investment flows intended to establish a commercial presence (mode 3) and of natural persons entering markets to supply a service (mode 4). Commitments under the relevant modes may enhance an economy's attractiveness for internationally mobile resources (human and/or physical capital) which, in turn, could help to overcome domestic supply shortages. It cannot be taken for granted that the requests received from trading partners, if any, coincide with an economy's developmental needs in attracting such resources.

Focal areas of interest, from a developmental perspective, might include infrastructural services, such as transport, distribution, finance and communications, that have economy-wide growth and efficiency implications. This implies, in turn, that in defining negotiating positions any defensive interests of sector incumbents, and the possible cost of adjustment, would need to be balanced with such wider economic benefits.

Liberalization strategies must be well conceived. For example, governments may need to think about the sequencing of individual reform steps within and between sectors, and the need for complementary regulatory change (definition of prudential standards, creation of supervisory bodies, etc.).

IDENTIFYING RELEVANT TRADING PARTNERS, SECTORS AND MODES

As in traditional GATT rounds, governments may seek the assistance of private-sector associations in identifying commercially promising export markets and defining negotiating interests. The need for consultations may be even greater in services than in merchandise trade, given the broad modal coverage of the GATS – possibly implying that active and defensive interests overlap within the same sector – and the dearth of detailed trade statistics and market information.

Brand recognition and goodwill are particularly important marketing factors in services trade. Potential customers tend to prefer well-known and -established suppliers since it is particularly difficult in services, given their non-tangible nature, to assess the quality of individual product. Potentially interesting export destinations therefore include markets or countries

(a) where nationals move for post-secondary education and training;
(b) to which nationals have emigrated; or
(c) with which close trade and investment links exist.

These destinations may be the same as for merchandise trade. Available evidence suggests, however, that services exports are generally destined for a broader range of markets.

A variety of sources may help to identify potentially interesting sectors and modes, including background papers prepared by the WTO Secretariat in 1998 and 1999 as well as a broad range of negotiating proposals tabled by both developed and developing countries since early 2000. They are all available on the WTO website. The background papers cover, *inter alia*,

> accountancy services
> advertising services
> architecture and engineering
> audiovisual services
> construction
> distribution services
> education services
> energy services
> environmental services
> financial services
> health and social services
> land and maritime transport services
> telecommunication services
> tourism services
> modes 1, 2 and 3
> mode 4

The papers have been compiled in a WTO Secretariat publication, *Guide to the GATS: An Overview of Issues for Further Liberalization of Trade in Services* (2000).

Many service firms rely on personal contacts and/or the existence of branches or representative offices to disseminate information and to advise (potential) clients abroad. Policies restricting temporary entry under mode 4 or commercial incorporation under mode 3 may thus have ramifications relating to trade under other modes as well. A broader perspective may be warranted, keeping in mind not only the importance of commercial presence and the presence of natural persons, but also of e-commerce as a potential substitute, in particular in the case of small and occasional exporters.

The International Trade Centre's *GATS Consultation Kit* can be helpful in structuring the domestic consultation process.

TECHNICAL ASPECTS OF REQUESTS

Requests may be addressed to a group of participants or to an individual Member. There are possibly four relevant targets, which are not mutually exclusive:

   (i) The addition of sectors that are not included in the relevant schedule.

   (ii) The removal of existing limitations or reductions in their restrictiveness (e.g. increases in the number of admitted suppliers or the levels of foreign equity participation). A request may also seek to transform an "unbound" into a commitment with or without limitations. Such requests always relate to measures affecting market access (Article XVI) or national treatment (Article XVII).

   (iii) The inscription of additional commitments (Article XVIII) relating to matters not falling within the scope of Articles XVI and XVII. A case in point is the Reference Paper on regulatory principles in basic telecommunications; a relatively high number of such requests were made, and implemented, during the extended negotiations under the Fourth Protocol.

   (iv) The removal of MFN exemptions. Paragraph 6 of the Annex on Article II (MFN) exemptions provides that existing exemptions be subject to negotiations in successive rounds of negotiations.

A request may be presented in the format of a simple letter. Thus, if a participant seeks a full commitment under Articles XVI or XVII, it would simply request that "none" be inscribed in the schedule of its trading partner(s).

Additional commitments under Article XVIII may need to be technically more specific. The article merely provides a framework for scheduling commitments on matters not falling under market access or national treatment. As evidenced by the telecommunications Reference Paper, such commitments may extend to areas not even addressed within the GATS itself, such as the establishment of an independent regulator. If a request is made to undertake such obligations not defined in the GATS, these must be described in accurate legal terms.

The process of exchanging requests tends to be purely bilateral in nature, without involving the WTO Secretariat. There was a suggestion at one stage in the Uruguay Round that when a request is made, a copy should also be sent to the Secretariat for its records. However, that practice was followed only for a short period of time.

TECHNICAL ASPECTS OF OFFERS

Offers would normally address the same issues as listed above, that is the addition of new sectors; the removal of existing limitations or the binding of modes not currently committed; the undertaking of additional commitments under Article XVIII; and the termination of MFN exemptions. Participants would take into account all requests received, after careful assessment of growth, developmental and other relevant policy implications.

While requests are usually presented in the form of a letter, an offer normally consists of a draft schedule of commitments. Therefore offers do require considerable technical preparation. In the Uruguay Round, in the absence of pre-existing schedules of commitments, participants started the negotiating process with the submission of offers. These were followed by requests, amended offers and so forth.

In the new round, offers will be submitted against the backdrop of existing schedules. The technical implications are currently being discussed in the Council for Trade in Services and the Committee on Specific Commitments. For these discussions Members expressed a preference for using, as a starting-point, consolidated schedules that incorporate not only the Uruguay Round outcome, but any later amendments and extensions, including those resulting from the negotiations on basic telecommunications and financial services. The modifications offered in current negotiations would be indicated through deletions, bolded insertions, italics or other agreed methods. The draft offer(s) would constitute negotiating document(s) with no legal status and would have no binding effects on the participant concerned. At that point Members might also wish to introduce technical clarifications to existing commitments.

In the future course of the negotiations there would be a succession of requests and offers. The initial offers, to be submitted by 31 March 2003, will be subject to revisions in response mainly to new or renewed requests. The offers are traditionally circulated multilaterally. This is useful not only for transparency purposes, but also from a functional point of view. While offers reflect the requests received (and, possibly, autonomous policy choices), they need to be open to consultation and negotiation by all partners.

With the submission of offers, participants enter a decisive stage of the negotiating process. Many governments send delegations to Geneva to conduct a long schedule of bilaterals with other delegations. Less time will be spent in Council or Committee meetings.

As an offshoot from the bilateral process, substantive issues of common interest might arise and require further multilateral discussion. For example, participants may want to address regulatory issues via Article XVIII, to clarify further concepts and disciplines contained in the GATS or to improve existing sector classifications. The Reference Paper in basic telecommunications, inscribed under Article XVIII, may stimulate work in other sectors facing similar problems of network access and market dominance, such as rail transport or electricity distribution. Other regulatory issues, such as transparency requirements, may be addressed as well. The development of a reference paper should essentially be open to all participants. Of course, once adopted or agreed upon, the paper takes legal effect only if it is incorporated in a Member's schedule.

8

MISCONCEPTIONS ABOUT THE GATS

SOURCES OF CRITICISM . . .

Civil society representatives have repeatedly voiced concerns about public policy implications of the GATS. Such concerns revolve, *inter alia*, around the Agreement's perceived impact on governments' ability to regulate socially important services and ensure equitable access across regions and population groups. It has been alleged that the concept of progressive liberalization, combined with the commercialization of some public services in individual countries, could result in subjecting core governmental activities to external (multilateral) disciplines. There have also been assertions that the Agreement contravenes basic notions of national sovereignty, requiring governments against their will to liberalize access and/or to accept constraints on socially motivated subsidy schemes. While some of these claims may be dismissed as scaremongering, driven for example by income interests of sector incumbents, the complexity of the GATS and the absence, in potentially relevant areas, of authoritative legal interpretations may have added a sense of uncertainty.

In response, the WTO Secretariat has authored, or contributed to, several publications explaining the structure and functioning of the Agreement and, by the same token, debunking frequently traded myths. Relevant sources include a Special Study, *Market Access: Unfinished Business*, a brief booklet, *GATS: Fact and Fiction*, and a Joint Study with the WHO, *WTO Agreements & Public Health*.

. . . AND THE FACTS

First and foremost, it may be worth reiterating one of the core concepts of the Agreement, the distinction between services liberalization and deregulation. Domestic regulations are not considered as barriers to market access and national treatment under the GATS and, therefore, are not subjected to trade negotiations. No WTO Member has ever questioned this basic tenet. Moreover, there are various exemption clauses in the Agreement, including Articles XII, XIV and XIV *bis*, that allow governments to ignore their obligations in specified circumstances with a view, for example, to protecting public security or life and health. The Secretariat is not aware of any cases to date where these provisions proved insufficient to address legitimate policy interests.

Should a Member feel the need to withdraw or modify its market access and national treatment obligations in a given sector, procedures are available under Article XXI. At the request of affected trading partners, the modifying Member is required to negotiate any necessary compensatory adjustment and, if unsuccessful, to accept arbitration. These procedures have been invoked only recently, more than eight years after the Agreement's entry into force. In turn, this testifies to the continued scope for political flexibility, despite the existence of scheduled commitments, in critical circumstances.

Services provided in the exercise of governmental authority are fully exempt from coverage. No changes are envisaged in the new round; the Negotiating Guidelines and Procedures, in document S/L/93, explicitly provide that the existing structure and principles of the GATS shall be respected. Moreover, there is evidence to date that the coexistence of public and private supplies within the same sector could have undermined the exemption of government service from the Agreement pursuant to Article I:3. Members have not apparently encountered any problems in this regard.

Consensus is the basic decision-making principle in the WTO. Like the GATT or the TRIPS Agreement, the GATS thus poses no risk to national sovereignty. It is simply not possible in negotiations within the purview of WTO to outvote a Member and/or subject it to disciplines that it is not prepared to accept. Moreover, it is worth bearing in mind that, as a last resort, nothing would prevent a frustrated government from quitting the Organization altogether. However, this has not happened to date. On the contrary, GATT/WTO membership has continued to prove highly attractive. Since the conclusion of the Tokyo Round in 1979, it has increased by about a half to close to 150 Members at present, and many more governments have applied for accession.

COMPLEXITY AS A CHALLENGE

The GATS is structurally more complex than the GATT. Among the most conspicuous differences are the existence of four modes of supply and of two distinct legal parameters – market access and national treatment – to determine conditions of market entry and participation. Thus, while a tariff schedule under GATT, in its simplest form, displays one tariff rate by sector, all specific commitments under the GATS consist of at least eight inscriptions, four each under market access and national treatment. This relatively complex structure is intended to enable Members to accommodate sector- or mode-specific constraints that they may encounter in the scheduling process and to liberalize progressively their services trade in line with their national policy objectives and levels of development. Complexity can thus be viewed, in part, as a precondition for effectiveness and flexibility.

Nevertheless, national administrations, in particular in small developing countries, may harbour doubts. From their perspective, the complexity of the Agreement implies a formidable negotiating challenge. It not only complicates internal decision-making and consultation procedures with other ministries and the private sector, but commands more attention (and resources) in the interpretation of requests received from, and the preparation of offers to be sent to, trading partners.

The Agreement seeks to address such concerns. First, it expressly recognizes the situation of developing countries and provides individual Members with "appropriate flexibility" for opening fewer sectors and liberalizing fewer types of transactions in line with their development situation. While these provisions in Article XIX:2 may have been intended mainly to protect developing countries from overly ambitious commitments that, especially in the absence of appropriate regulatory frameworks, may cause excessive adjustment pains, they also protect from undue negotiating pressure across too wide a range of sectors and policy areas. Moreover, Article XXV of the GATS expressly recognizes the need for the WTO Secretariat to provide technical assistance to developing countries. The Article needs to be read in conjunction with the Negotiating Guidelines and Procedures of March 2001 and, even more important, the Doha Ministerial Declaration of November 2001. The Declaration further emphasizes, and elaborates on, the role and necessity of technical co-operation and capacity building (paras. 38–41).

APPENDIX 1
UNDERSTANDING YOUR COUNTRY'S SERVICES TRADE

The Importance of Services for Consumers and Producers, Traders and Investors

Services are an important input for virtually all commercial activities, including other services, and a core determinant of the quality of life. No economy or social community could prosper without adequate transportation, communication, education or health services.

Developed and developing economies have built competitive service industries – the most visible in developing countries include tourism, construction and transport – and benefit from the efficiency of a modern service infrastructure. Services exports may constitute an important foreign-currency earner and contribute to overall economic expansion. The attendant employment effects could help to stem migration from less developed regions and provide a nucleus for self-sustained growth.

The quality of available business services may prove crucial to development. Research in Latin America in the 1980s by UNCTAD indicated that one of the primary distinctions between developed and developing economies was the availability of highly specialized business services. More recent research in Asia, Africa and the Middle East has confirmed the importance of business services of international quality that are customized according to local commercial needs. By tapping into

---

Food for thought
 (i) Name services sectors that contribute directly to the competitiveness of your country's goods producers.
 (ii) Name sectors whose quality and cost-effectiveness is of particular interest to potential investors.

Possible reply
 (i) Infrastructural services that provide direct inputs such as telecommunications, transport, energy, banking, insurance, distribution;
    business services such as accountancy, management consulting, and legal services;
    services that enhance quality and efficiency of the workforce (e.g. education and health).
 (ii) All of the above, with particular emphasis on infrastructral services.

---

regional or global markets, local service firms are able to support the development of specialized expertise.

To ensure compliance with prevailing quality standards and social preferences, governments around the world have issued services-related regulations, including licensing and certification requirements or universal access obligations for essential supplies.

Identifying Current Services Exports and Imports

Services trade is in large part invisible and thus tends to be underestimated. Nevertheless, on average across all countries, service firms are earning at least 20 per cent, running up to over 90 per cent in individual cases, of foreign exchange. Some service suppliers are even unaware of their exports, especially if they trade mostly under mode 2 (i.e. services sales to foreigners visiting the country as tourists, students or patients, or to domestically established, but foreign-owned companies). Moreover, the services content of manufacturing trade, including services as diverse as finance, insurance, transport or logistics, seem to have increased significantly over time. Subject to various heroic assumptions, the share of individual modes in world services trade covered by GATS has recently been estimated at

> less than 30 per cent for mode 1;
> close to 15 per cent for mode 2;
> over 50 per cent for mode 3; and
> some 1 or 2 per cent for mode 4.[1]

Domestic Consultations

The majority of WTO Members have already participated in negotiating rounds under the GATT and have experience in identifying and addressing the concerns of goods exporters. By contrast, since the GATS is a young agreement, there is a smaller base of experience from which to identify and pursue trade interests in services, and statistical information is far more patchy. Services trade statistics have historically been incomplete, in part because there is not a convenient checkpoint (such as a border crossing) and most countries lack a registry of service exporters.

Second, since very many service firms are small or very small, they are likely to be under-represented in statistical surveys due to response burden. In addition, very small firms typically do not have staff dedicated to government relations, and they may have had little motivation to date to get more actively involved, since services agreements as yet offer few actual benefits to private firms (other than transparency).

---

[1] *Source*: Trade in Services Section of Statistics Division, WTO Secretariat.

Table A1. *Sample List of Potential Participants**

Category	Potential participant
Business services	Professional services associations
	Professional licensing registrars
	Service industry associations
	Real estate board
	National research agency
Communication services	Service industry associations
	Telecommunications regulator
	National film agency
	National news service
Construction	Construction association
	Engineering association
	Architectural association
	Housing authority
	Environmental impact
	Safety standards
Distribution	Retailers' association
	Wholesalers' association
	Importers' association
	Franchise association
	Duty-free shops
Educational services	Association of private schools
	Association of community colleges
	Career guidance association
	Parent-teachers' association
	Student association
Environmental services	Environmental services association
	Environmental impact
Financial services	Bankers' association
	Brokers' association
	Insurance association
	Central bank
	Security exchange/stock market
	Securities regulator
Health and social services	Hospital association
	Outpatient clinics association
	Mental health association
	Health advocates
	Social welfare advocates

(cont.)

Table A1. (*cont.*)

Category	Potential participant
Recreation, sport, culture	Major sports team managers National museum National library and archives National performing arts groups Council for the arts
Tourism and travel	Travel agencies association Tour guides association Hotel association Restaurant association Parks authority Environmental impact
Transport	Airport authority Air traffic controllers' association Port authority Vehicle licensing authority
Other: energy services	Utility regulator
All sectors	Independent research and advisory bodies and agencies (research departments of central banks, academic community, international organizations, etc.) Unions

*Adapted from OECD, 2002.

In order to negotiate effectively, Members need to identify their main services markets, to develop a vision of future trading and growth opportunities and to assess the impact of various liberalization strategies on the sectors concerned and, even more importantly, on overall economic and social development. Consultations with independent experts and various stakeholders may contribute greatly to this process. They would include not only the business community, that is producers, importers and commercial users of services, but non-profit organizations representing consumer and other interests, and the economic research community. Before useful consultations can take place, participants need to be informed about the GATS.

It is important to ensure that the domestic decision-making process is not distorted by vested interests that may have been created under traditional trade regimes. It would be of little surprise, for example, if market incumbents that have long been shielded from import and domestic competition express a strong preference for perpetuating the status quo. Industry consultations should thus form part of a broader information-gathering and evaluation process. Promising strides have recently been taken in promoting cross-country research networks in various regions of the world, including sub-Saharan Africa (e.g. the African Economic Research Consortium or the Southern Africa Trade Research Network), with a view to providing independent inputs for decision-making and putting trade policies into a wider developmental context.

As a potential source of inspiration, Table A1 provides a listing of potential contributors to the consultation process, apart from the producers and agencies directly involved.

Effective consultation is an ongoing, two-way process, whereby participants provide inputs and receive feedback. In order to be useful for negotiations, the consultations will need to proceed as much as possible by sector, mode of supply and, for the formulation of negotiating requests, export market. To help with this process, the International Trade Centre UNCTAD/WTO has published a "GATS Consultation Kit", which can be found online at www.intracen.org.

APPENDIX 2
RELEVANT SERVICES STATISTICS AND CLASSIFICATIONS

The ultimate purpose of trade liberalization, in whatever sectoral context, lies in its contribution to growth and development. Unfortunately, this contribution is far more difficult to trace than the immediate impact, not always positive, on the industries most directly affected. This is a particular concern in infrastructural services, which in many countries have long been protected from competition – to the apparent benefit of the service providers directly involved and, potentially, at the expense of overall economic expansion. However, it is not only the growth and efficiency effects that are difficult to capture; information gaps already exist at the sector level.

Given the non-tangible nature of many services, sector-specific trade data are more patchy than we are used to in agriculture, mining or manufacturing. (There may be some exceptions, such as transportat and tourism, where volume indicators are readily available.) However, the situation is gradually improving, owing in part to the impetus provided by the conclusion of GATS. After years of preparation, under the auspices of the United Nations Statistical Office (UNSO), the *Manual of Statistics on International Trade in Services* was completed in early 2002 (see www.un.org/Depts/unsd/class/techgrp.htm).

The manual extends the balance-of-payments-based definition of international services trade to reflect the four modes of supply. In particular, a new international framework – Foreign Affiliate Trade in Services statistics – provides guidance on the measurement of services provided through foreign-owned firms in host-country markets. Nevertheless, the manual builds on and maintains consistency with existing frameworks, including the IMF *Balance of Payments Manual*, fifth edition (BPM5).

Current data problems are attributable in part to the novelty of the GATS definition of services trade and to a lack of information (or interest) on the part of the companies involved. Service suppliers are often unaware of their export activities in situations where they sell, for example, to foreigners visiting the country. By the same token, the services "imported" via foreign commercial presence, for example the turnover in their host countries of foreign-owned telecom companies, banks, hotels and so on, have long escaped statistical coverage.

For the purposes of the Uruguay Round negotiations, the WTO Secretariat developed a services sector classification with a view to ensuring cross-country comparability and consistency of the commitments undertaken (MTN.GNS/W/120). Although optional, most Members followed this classification, which, in some sectors (maritime transport, financial services, telecommunications) was complemented by alternative models. As far as possible, the 160-odd sub-sectors of which W/120 is composed are defined as aggregates of the more detailed categories contained in the United Nations provisional Central Product Classification (CPC). Recourse to CPC categories helps to improve clarity over the scope of the commitments actually undertaken; for each sector number, the CPC provides a brief description of what is actually covered.

ANNEX
GENERAL AGREEMENT ON TRADE IN SERVICES

GENERAL AGREEMENT ON TRADE IN SERVICES

Members,

Recognizing the growing importance of trade in services for the growth and development of the world economy;

Wishing to establish a multilateral framework of principles and rules for trade in services with a view to the expansion of such trade under conditions of transparency and progressive liberalization and as a means of promoting the economic growth of all trading partners and the development of developing countries;

Desiring the early achievement of progressively higher levels of liberalization of trade in services through successive rounds of multilateral negotiations aimed at promoting the interests of all participants on a mutually advantageous basis and at securing an overall balance of rights and obligations, while giving due respect to national policy objectives;

Recognizing the right of Members to regulate, and to introduce new regulations, on the supply of services within their territories in order to meet national policy objectives and, given asymmetries existing with respect to the degree of development of services regulations in different countries, the particular need of developing countries to exercise this right;

Desiring to facilitate the increasing participation of developing countries in trade in services and the expansion of their service exports including, *inter alia*, through the strengthening of their domestic services capacity and its efficiency and competitiveness;

Taking particular account of the serious difficulty of the least-developed countries in view of their special economic situation and their development, trade and financial needs;

Hereby *agree* as follows:

PART I
SCOPE AND DEFINITION

Article I

Scope and Definition

1.   This Agreement applies to measures by Members affecting trade in services.

2.   For the purposes of this Agreement, trade in services is defined as the supply of a service:

   (a)   from the territory of one Member into the territory of any other Member;
   (b)   in the territory of one Member to the service consumer of any other Member;
   (c)   by a service supplier of one Member, through commercial presence in the territory of any other Member;
   (d)   by a service supplier of one Member, through presence of natural persons of a Member in the territory of any other Member.

3.   For the purposes of this Agreement:

   (a)   "measures by Members" means measures taken by:
      (i)   central, regional or local governments and authorities; and
      (ii)   non-governmental bodies in the exercise of powers delegated by central, regional or local governments or authorities;
      In fulfilling its obligations and commitments under the Agreement, each Member shall take such reasonable measures as may be available to it to ensure their observance by regional and local governments and authorities and non-governmental bodies within its territory;
   (b)   "services" includes any service in any sector except services supplied in the exercise of governmental authority;
   (c)   "a service supplied in the exercise of governmental authority" means any service which is supplied neither on a commercial basis, nor in competition with one or more service suppliers.

PART II
GENERAL OBLIGATIONS AND DISCIPLINES

Article II

Most-Favoured-Nation Treatment

1.   With respect to any measure covered by this Agreement, each Member shall accord immediately and unconditionally to services and service suppliers of any other Member treatment no less favourable than that it accords to like services and service suppliers of any other country.

2.   A Member may maintain a measure inconsistent with paragraph 1 provided that such a measure is listed in, and meets the conditions of, the Annex on Article II Exemptions.

3.   The provisions of this Agreement shall not be so construed as to prevent any Member from conferring or according advantages to adjacent countries in order to facilitate exchanges limited to contiguous frontier zones of services that are both locally produced and consumed.

Article III

Transparency

1.   Each Member shall publish promptly and, except in emergency situations, at the latest by the time of their entry into force, all relevant measures of general application which pertain to or affect the operation of this Agreement. International agreements pertaining to or affecting trade in services to which a Member is a signatory shall also be published.

2.   Where publication as referred to in paragraph 1 is not practicable, such information shall be made otherwise publicly available.

3.   Each Member shall promptly and at least annually inform the Council for Trade in Services of the introduction of any new, or any changes to existing, laws, regulations or administrative guidelines which significantly affect trade in services covered by its specific commitments under this Agreement.

4.   Each Member shall respond promptly to all requests by any other Member for specific information on any of its measures of general application or international agreements within the meaning of paragraph 1. Each Member shall also establish one or more enquiry points to provide specific information to other Members, upon request, on all such matters as well as those subject to the notification requirement in paragraph 3. Such enquiry points shall be established within two years from the date of entry into force of the Agreement Establishing the WTO (referred to in this Agreement as the "WTO Agreement"). Appropriate flexibility with respect to the time-limit within which such enquiry points are to be established may be agreed upon for individual developing country Members. Enquiry points need not be depositories of laws and regulations.

5.   Any Member may notify to the Council for Trade in Services any measure, taken by any other Member, which it considers affects the operation of this Agreement.

Article III bis

Disclosure of Confidential Information

Nothing in this Agreement shall require any Member to provide confidential information, the disclosure of which would impede law enforcement, or otherwise be contrary to the public interest, or which would prejudice legitimate commercial interests of particular enterprises, public or private.

Article IV

Increasing Participation of Developing Countries

1.   The increasing participation of developing country Members in world trade shall be facilitated through negotiated specific commitments, by different Members pursuant to Parts III and IV of this Agreement, relating to:

(a)   the strengthening of their domestic services capacity and its efficiency and competitiveness, *inter alia* through access to technology on a commercial basis;

(b)   the improvement of their access to distribution channels and information networks; and

(c)   the liberalization of market access in sectors and modes of supply of export interest to them.

2.   Developed country Members, and to the extent possible other Members, shall establish contact points within two years from the date of entry into force of the WTO Agreement to facilitate the access of developing country Members' service suppliers to information, related to their respective markets, concerning:

(a)   commercial and technical aspects of the supply of services;

(b)   registration, recognition and obtaining of professional qualifications; and

(c)   the availability of services technology.

3.   Special priority shall be given to the least-developed country Members in the implementation of paragraphs 1 and 2. Particular account shall be taken of the serious difficulty of the least-developed countries in accepting negotiated specific commitments in view of their special economic situation and their development, trade and financial needs.

Article V

Economic Integration

1.   This Agreement shall not prevent any of its Members from being a party to or entering into an agreement liberalizing trade in services between or among the parties to such an agreement, provided that such an agreement:

(a)   has substantial sectoral coverage[1], and

(b)   provides for the absence or elimination of substantially all discrimination, in the sense of Article XVII, between or among the parties, in the sectors covered under subparagraph (a), through:

(i)   elimination of existing discriminatory measures, and/or

(ii)   prohibition of new or more discriminatory measures,

---

[1]   This condition is understood in terms of number of sectors, volume of trade affected and modes of supply. In order to meet this condition, agreements should not provide for the *a priori* exclusion of any mode of supply.

either at the entry into force of that agreement or on the basis of a reasonable time-frame, except for measures permitted under Articles XI, XII, XIV and XIV *bis*.

2. In evaluating whether the conditions under paragraph 1(b) are met, consideration may be given to the relationship of the agreement to a wider process of economic integration or trade liberalization among the countries concerned.

3. (a) Where developing countries are parties to an agreement of the type referred to in paragraph 1, flexibility shall be provided for regarding the conditions set out in paragraph 1, particularly with reference to subparagraph (b) thereof, in accordance with the level of development of the countries concerned, both overall and in individual sectors and subsectors.

    (b) Notwithstanding paragraph 6, in the case of an agreement of the type referred to in paragraph 1 involving only developing countries, more favourable treatment may be granted to juridical persons owned or controlled by natural persons of the parties to such an agreement.

4. Any agreement referred to in paragraph 1 shall be designed to facilitate trade between the parties to the agreement and shall not in respect of any Member outside the agreement raise the overall level of barriers to trade in services within the respective sectors or subsectors compared to the level applicable prior to such an agreement.

5. If, in the conclusion, enlargement or any significant modification of any agreement under paragraph 1, a Member intends to withdraw or modify a specific commitment inconsistently with the terms and conditions set out in its Schedule, it shall provide at least 90 days advance notice of such modification or withdrawal and the procedure set forth in paragraphs 2, 3 and 4 of Article XXI shall apply.

6. A service supplier of any other Member that is a juridical person constituted under the laws of a party to an agreement referred to in paragraph 1 shall be entitled to treatment granted under such agreement, provided that it engages in substantive business operations in the territory of the parties to such agreement.

7. (a) Members which are parties to any agreement referred to in paragraph 1 shall promptly notify any such agreement and any enlargement or any significant modification of that agreement to the Council for Trade in Services. They shall also make available to the Council such relevant information as may be requested by it. The Council may establish a working party to examine such an agreement or enlargement or modification of that agreement and to report to the Council on its consistency with this Article.

    (b) Members which are parties to any agreement referred to in paragraph 1 which is implemented on the basis of a time-frame shall report periodically to the Council for Trade in Services on its implementation. The Council may establish a working party to examine such reports if it deems such a working party necessary.

(c) Based on the reports of the working parties referred to in subparagraphs (a) and (b), the Council may make recommendations to the parties as it deems appropriate.

8. A Member which is a party to any agreement referred to in paragraph 1 may not seek compensation for trade benefits that may accrue to any other Member from such agreement.

Article V bis

Labour Markets Integration Agreements

This Agreement shall not prevent any of its Members from being a party to an agreement establishing full integration[2] of the labour markets between or among the parties to such an agreement, provided that such an agreement:

(a) exempts citizens of parties to the agreement from requirements concerning residency and work permits;
(b) is notified to the Council for Trade in Services.

Article VI

Domestic Regulation

1. In sectors where specific commitments are undertaken, each Member shall ensure that all measures of general application affecting trade in services are administered in a reasonable, objective and impartial manner.

2. (a) Each Member shall maintain or institute as soon as practicable judicial, arbitral or administrative tribunals or procedures which provide, at the request of an affected service supplier, for the prompt review of, and where justified, appropriate remedies for, administrative decisions affecting trade in services. Where such procedures are not independent of the agency entrusted with the administrative decision concerned, the Member shall ensure that the procedures in fact provide for an objective and impartial review.

(b) The provisions of subparagraph (a) shall not be construed to require a Member to institute such tribunals or procedures where this would be inconsistent with its constitutional structure or the nature of its legal system.

3. Where authorization is required for the supply of a service on which a specific commitment has been made, the competent authorities of a Member shall, within a reasonable period of time after the submission of an application considered complete under domestic laws and regulations, inform the applicant of the decision concerning the application. At the request of the applicant, the competent

---

[2] Typically, such integration provides citizens of the parties concerned with a right of free entry to the employment markets of the parties and includes measures concerning conditions of pay, other conditions of employment and social benefits.

authorities of the Member shall provide, without undue delay, information concerning the status of the application.

4.   With a view to ensuring that measures relating to qualification requirements and procedures, technical standards and licensing requirements do not constitute unnecessary barriers to trade in services, the Council for Trade in Services shall, through appropriate bodies it may establish, develop any necessary disciplines. Such disciplines shall aim to ensure that such requirements are, *inter alia*:

(a)   based on objective and transparent criteria, such as competence and the ability to supply the service;

(b)   not more burdensome than necessary to ensure the quality of the service;

(c)   in the case of licensing procedures, not in themselves a restriction on the supply of the service.

5.   (a)   In sectors in which a Member has undertaken specific commitments, pending the entry into force of disciplines developed in these sectors pursuant to paragraph 4, the Member shall not apply licensing and qualification requirements and technical standards that nullify or impair such specific commitments in a manner which:

(i)   does not comply with the criteria outlined in subparagraphs 4(a), (b) or (c); and

(ii)   could not reasonably have been expected of that Member at the time the specific commitments in those sectors were made.

(b)   In determining whether a Member is in conformity with the obligation under paragraph 5(a), account shall be taken of international standards of relevant international organizations[3] applied by that Member.

6.   In sectors where specific commitments regarding professional services are undertaken, each Member shall provide for adequate procedures to verify the competence of professionals of any other Member.

Article VII

Recognition

1.   For the purposes of the fulfilment, in whole or in part, of its standards or criteria for the authorization, licensing or certification of services suppliers, and subject to the requirements of paragraph 3, a Member may recognize the education or experience obtained, requirements met, or licenses or certifications granted in a particular country. Such recognition, which may be achieved through harmonization or otherwise, may be based upon an agreement or arrangement with the country concerned or may be accorded autonomously.

2.   A Member that is a party to an agreement or arrangement of the type referred to in paragraph 1, whether existing or future, shall afford adequate opportunity

---

[3]   The term "relevant international organizations" refers to international bodies whose membership is open to the relevant bodies of at least all Members of the WTO.

for other interested Members to negotiate their accession to such an agreement or arrangement or to negotiate comparable ones with it. Where a Member accords recognition autonomously, it shall afford adequate opportunity for any other Member to demonstrate that education, experience, licenses, or certifications obtained or requirements met in that other Member's territory should be recognized.

3. A Member shall not accord recognition in a manner which would constitute a means of discrimination between countries in the application of its standards or criteria for the authorization, licensing or certification of services suppliers, or a disguised restriction on trade in services.

4. Each Member shall:

> (a) within 12 months from the date on which the WTO Agreement takes effect for it, inform the Council for Trade in Services of its existing recognition measures and state whether such measures are based on agreements or arrangements of the type referred to in paragraph 1;
>
> (b) promptly inform the Council for Trade in Services as far in advance as possible of the opening of negotiations on an agreement or arrangement of the type referred to in paragraph 1 in order to provide adequate opportunity to any other Member to indicate their interest in participating in the negotiations before they enter a substantive phase;
>
> (c) promptly inform the Council for Trade in Services when it adopts new recognition measures or significantly modifies existing ones and state whether the measures are based on an agreement or arrangement of the type referred to in paragraph 1.

5. Wherever appropriate, recognition should be based on multilaterally agreed criteria. In appropriate cases, Members shall work in cooperation with relevant intergovernmental and non-governmental organizations towards the establishment and adoption of common international standards and criteria for recognition and common international standards for the practice of relevant services trades and professions.

Article VIII

Monopolies and Exclusive Service Suppliers

1. Each Member shall ensure that any monopoly supplier of a service in its territory does not, in the supply of the monopoly service in the relevant market, act in a manner inconsistent with that Member's obligations under Article II and specific commitments.

2. Where a Member's monopoly supplier competes, either directly or through an affiliated company, in the supply of a service outside the scope of its monopoly rights and which is subject to that Member's specific commitments, the Member shall ensure that such a supplier does not abuse its monopoly position to act in its territory in a manner inconsistent with such commitments.

3. The Council for Trade in Services may, at the request of a Member which has a reason to believe that a monopoly supplier of a service of any other Member is acting

in a manner inconsistent with paragraph 1 or 2, request the Member establishing, maintaining or authorizing such supplier to provide specific information concerning the relevant operations.

4.   If, after the date of entry into force of the WTO Agreement, a Member grants monopoly rights regarding the supply of a service covered by its specific commitments, that Member shall notify the Council for Trade in Services no later than three months before the intended implementation of the grant of monopoly rights and the provisions of paragraphs 2, 3 and 4 of Article XXI shall apply.

5.   The provisions of this Article shall also apply to cases of exclusive service suppliers, where a Member, formally or in effect, (*a*) authorizes or establishes a small number of service suppliers and (*b*) substantially prevents competition among those suppliers in its territory.

Article IX

Business Practices

1.   Members recognize that certain business practices of service suppliers, other than those falling under Article VIII, may restrain competition and thereby restrict trade in services.

2.   Each Member shall, at the request of any other Member, enter into consultations with a view to eliminating practices referred to in paragraph 1. The Member addressed shall accord full and sympathetic consideration to such a request and shall cooperate through the supply of publicly available non-confidential information of relevance to the matter in question. The Member addressed shall also provide other information available to the requesting Member, subject to its domestic law and to the conclusion of satisfactory agreement concerning the safeguarding of its confidentiality by the requesting Member.

Article X

Emergency Safeguard Measures

1.   There shall be multilateral negotiations on the question of emergency safeguard measures based on the principle of non-discrimination. The results of such negotiations shall enter into effect on a date not later than three years from the date of entry into force of the WTO Agreement.

2.   In the period before the entry into effect of the results of the negotiations referred to in paragraph 1, any Member may, notwithstanding the provisions of paragraph 1 of Article XXI, notify the Council on Trade in Services of its intention to modify or withdraw a specific commitment after a period of one year from the date on which the commitment enters into force; provided that the Member shows cause to the Council that the modification or withdrawal cannot await the lapse of the three-year period provided for in paragraph 1 of Article XXI.

3.   The provisions of paragraph 2 shall cease to apply three years after the date of entry into force of the WTO Agreement.

Article XI

Payments and Transfers

1.   Except under the circumstances envisaged in Article XII, a Member shall not apply restrictions on international transfers and payments for current transactions relating to its specific commitments.

2.   Nothing in this Agreement shall affect the rights and obligations of the members of the International Monetary Fund under the Articles of Agreement of the Fund, including the use of exchange actions which are in conformity with the Articles of Agreement, provided that a Member shall not impose restrictions on any capital transactions inconsistently with its specific commitments regarding such transactions, except under Article XII or at the request of the Fund.

Article XII

Restrictions to Safeguard the Balance of Payments

1.   In the event of serious balance-of-payments and external financial difficulties or threat thereof, a Member may adopt or maintain restrictions on trade in services on which it has undertaken specific commitments, including on payments or transfers for transactions related to such commitments.   It is recognized that particular pressures on the balance of payments of a Member in the process of economic development or economic transition may necessitate the use of restrictions to ensure, *inter alia,* the maintenance of a level of financial reserves adequate for the implementation of its programme of economic development or economic transition.

2.   The restrictions referred to in paragraph 1:

   (a)   shall not discriminate among Members;
   (b)   shall be consistent with the Articles of Agreement of the International Monetary Fund;
   (c)   shall avoid unnecessary damage to the commercial, economic and financial interests of any other Member;
   (d)   shall not exceed those necessary to deal with the circumstances described in paragraph 1;
   (e)   shall be temporary and be phased out progressively as the situation specified in paragraph 1 improves.

3.   In determining the incidence of such restrictions, Members may give priority to the supply of services which are more essential to their economic or development programmes.   However, such restrictions shall not be adopted or maintained for the purpose of protecting a particular service sector.

4.   Any restrictions adopted or maintained under paragraph 1, or any changes therein, shall be promptly notified to the General Council.

5.   (a)   Members applying the provisions of this Article shall consult promptly with the Committee on Balance-of-Payments Restrictions on restrictions adopted under this Article.

(b) The Ministerial Conference shall establish procedures[4] for periodic consultations with the objective of enabling such recommendations to be made to the Member concerned as it may deem appropriate.

(c) Such consultations shall assess the balance-of-payment situation of the Member concerned and the restrictions adopted or maintained under this Article, taking into account, *inter alia*, such factors as:

(i) the nature and extent of the balance-of-payments and the external financial difficulties;

(ii) the external economic and trading environment of the consulting Member;

(iii) alternative corrective measures which may be available.

(d) The consultations shall address the compliance of any restrictions with paragraph 2, in particular the progressive phaseout of restrictions in accordance with paragraph 2(e).

(e) In such consultations, all findings of statistical and other facts presented by the International Monetary Fund relating to foreign exchange, monetary reserves and balance of payments, shall be accepted and conclusions shall be based on the assessment by the Fund of the balance-of-payments and the external financial situation of the consulting Member.

6.   If a Member which is not a member of the International Monetary Fund wishes to apply the provisions of this Article, the Ministerial Conference shall establish a review procedure and any other procedures necessary.

Article XIII

Government Procurement

1.   Articles II, XVI and XVII shall not apply to laws, regulations or requirements governing the procurement by governmental agencies of services purchased for governmental purposes and not with a view to commercial resale or with a view to use in the supply of services for commercial sale.

2.   There shall be multilateral negotiations on government procurement in services under this Agreement within two years from the date of entry into force of the WTO Agreement.

Article XIV

General Exceptions

Subject to the requirement that such measures are not applied in a manner which would constitute a means of arbitrary or unjustifiable discrimination between countries where like conditions prevail, or a disguised restriction on trade in services, nothing in this Agreement shall be construed to prevent the adoption or enforcement by any Member of measures:

---

[4] It is understood that the procedures under paragraph 5 shall be the same as the GATT 1994 procedures.

(a) necessary to protect public morals or to maintain public order;[5]

(b) necessary to protect human, animal or plant life or health;

(c) necessary to secure compliance with laws or regulations which are not inconsistent with the provisions of this Agreement including those relating to:

  (i) the prevention of deceptive and fraudulent practices or to deal with the effects of a default on services contracts;

  (ii) the protection of the privacy of individuals in relation to the processing and dissemination of personal data and the protection of confidentiality of individual records and accounts;

  (iii) safety;

(d) inconsistent with Article XVII, provided that the difference in treatment is aimed at ensuring the equitable or effective[6] imposition or collection of direct taxes in respect of services or service suppliers of other Members;

(e) inconsistent with Article II, provided that the difference in treatment is the result of an agreement on the avoidance of double taxation or provisions on the avoidance of double taxation in any other international agreement or arrangement by which the Member is bound.

Article XIV bis

Security Exceptions

1. Nothing in this Agreement shall be construed:

  (a) to require any Member to furnish any information, the disclosure of which it considers contrary to its essential security interests; or

---

[5] The public order exception may be invoked only where a genuine and sufficiently serious threat is posed to one of the fundamental interests of society.

[6] Measures that are aimed at ensuring the equitable or effective imposition or collection of direct taxes include measures taken by a Member under its taxation system which:

  (i) apply to non-resident service suppliers in recognition of the fact that the tax obligation of non-residents is determined with respect to taxable items sourced or located in the Member's territory; or

  (ii) apply to non-residents in order to ensure the imposition or collection of taxes in the Member's territory; or

  (iii) apply to non-residents or residents in order to prevent the avoidance or evasion of taxes, including compliance measures; or

  (iv) apply to consumers of services supplied in or from the territory of another Member in order to ensure the imposition or collection of taxes on such consumers derived from sources in the Member's territory; or

  (v) distinguish service suppliers subject to tax on worldwide taxable items from other service suppliers, in recognition of the difference in the nature of the tax base between them; or

  (vi) determine, allocate or apportion income, profit, gain, loss, deduction or credit of resident persons or branches, or between related persons or branches of the same person, in order to safeguard the Member's tax base.

Tax terms or concepts in paragraph (d) of Article XIV and in this footnote are determined according to tax definitions and concepts, or equivalent or similar definitions and concepts, under the domestic law of the Member taking the measure.

(b) to prevent any Member from taking any action which it considers necessary for the protection of its essential security interests:

(i) relating to the supply of services as carried out directly or indirectly for the purpose of provisioning a military establishment;

(ii) relating to fissionable and fusionable materials or the materials from which they are derived;

(iii) taken in time of war or other emergency in international relations; or

(c) to prevent any Member from taking any action in pursuance of its obligations under the United Nations Charter for the maintenance of international peace and security.

2. The Council for Trade in Services shall be informed to the fullest extent possible of measures taken under paragraphs 1(b) and (c) and of their termination.

Article XV

Subsidies

1. Members recognize that, in certain circumstances, subsidies may have distortive effects on trade in services. Members shall enter into negotiations with a view to developing the necessary multilateral disciplines to avoid such trade-distortive effects.[7] The negotiations shall also address the appropriateness of countervailing procedures. Such negotiations shall recognize the role of subsidies in relation to the development programmes of developing countries and take into account the needs of Members, particularly developing country Members, for flexibility in this area. For the purpose of such negotiations, Members shall exchange information concerning all subsidies related to trade in services that they provide to their domestic service suppliers.

2. Any Member which considers that it is adversely affected by a subsidy of another Member may request consultations with that Member on such matters. Such requests shall be accorded sympathetic consideration.

PART III
SPECIFIC COMMITMENTS

Article XVI

Market Access

1. With respect to market access through the modes of supply identified in Article I, each Member shall accord services and service suppliers of any other Member treatment no less favourable than that provided for under the terms, limitations and conditions agreed and specified in its Schedule.[8]

---

[7] A future work programme shall determine how, and in what time-frame, negotiations on such multilateral disciplines will be conducted.

[8] If a Member undertakes a market-access commitment in relation to the supply of a service through the mode of supply referred to in subparagraph 2(a) of Article I and if the cross-border movement of capital is an essential

2.   In sectors where market-access commitments are undertaken, the measures which a Member shall not maintain or adopt either on the basis of a regional subdivision or on the basis of its entire territory, unless otherwise specified in its Schedule, are defined as:

(a) limitations on the number of service suppliers whether in the form of numerical quotas, monopolies, exclusive service suppliers or the requirements of an economic needs test;

(b) limitations on the total value of service transactions or assets in the form of numerical quotas or the requirement of an economic needs test;

(c) limitations on the total number of service operations or on the total quantity of service output expressed in terms of designated numerical units in the form of quotas or the requirement of an economic needs test;[9]

(d) limitations on the total number of natural persons that may be employed in a particular service sector or that a service supplier may employ and who are necessary for, and directly related to, the supply of a specific service in the form of numerical quotas or the requirement of an economic needs test;

(e) measures which restrict or require specific types of legal entity or joint venture through which a service supplier may supply a service; and

(f) limitations on the participation of foreign capital in terms of maximum percentage limit on foreign shareholding or the total value of individual or aggregate foreign investment.

Article XVII

National Treatment

1.   In the sectors inscribed in its Schedule, and subject to any conditions and qualifications set out therein, each Member shall accord to services and service suppliers of any other Member, in respect of all measures affecting the supply of services, treatment no less favourable than that it accords to its own like services and service suppliers.[10]

2.   A Member may meet the requirement of paragraph 1 by according to services and service suppliers of any other Member, either formally identical treatment or formally different treatment to that it accords to its own like services and service suppliers.

3.   Formally identical or formally different treatment shall be considered to be less favourable if it modifies the conditions of competition in favour of services or

---

part of the service itself, that Member is thereby committed to allow such movement of capital. If a Member undertakes a market-access commitment in relation to the supply of a service through the mode of supply referred to in subparagraph 2(c) of Article I, it is thereby committed to allow related transfers of capital into its territory.

[9] Subparagraph 2(c) does not cover measures of a Member which limit inputs for the supply of services.

[10] Specific commitments assumed under this Article shall not be construed to require any Member to compensate for any inherent competitive disadvantages which result from the foreign character of the relevant services or service suppliers.

service suppliers of the Member compared to like services or service suppliers of any other Member.

Article XVIII

Additional Commitments

Members may negotiate commitments with respect to measures affecting trade in services not subject to scheduling under Articles XVI or XVII, including those regarding qualifications, standards or licensing matters. Such commitments shall be inscribed in a Member's Schedule.

PART IV
PROGRESSIVE LIBERALIZATION

Article XIX

Negotiation of Specific Commitments

1. In pursuance of the objectives of this Agreement, Members shall enter into successive rounds of negotiations, beginning not later than five years from the date of entry into force of the WTO Agreement and periodically thereafter, with a view to achieving a progressively higher level of liberalization. Such negotiations shall be directed to the reduction or elimination of the adverse effects on trade in services of measures as a means of providing effective market access. This process shall take place with a view to promoting the interests of all participants on a mutually advantageous basis and to securing an overall balance of rights and obligations.

2. The process of liberalization shall take place with due respect for national policy objectives and the level of development of individual Members, both overall and in individual sectors. There shall be appropriate flexibility for individual developing country Members for opening fewer sectors, liberalizing fewer types of transactions, progressively extending market access in line with their development situation and, when making access to their markets available to foreign service suppliers, attaching to such access conditions aimed at achieving the objectives referred to in Article IV.

3. For each round, negotiating guidelines and procedures shall be established. For the purposes of establishing such guidelines, the Council for Trade in Services shall carry out an assessment of trade in services in overall terms and on a sectoral basis with reference to the objectives of this Agreement, including those set out in paragraph 1 of Article IV. Negotiating guidelines shall establish modalities for the treatment of liberalization undertaken autonomously by Members since previous negotiations, as well as for the special treatment for least-developed country Members under the provisions of paragraph 3 of Article IV.

4. The process of progressive liberalization shall be advanced in each such round through bilateral, plurilateral or multilateral negotiations directed towards increasing the general level of specific commitments undertaken by Members under this Agreement.

Article XX

Schedules of Specific Commitments

1.   Each Member shall set out in a schedule the specific commitments it undertakes under Part III of this Agreement. With respect to sectors where such commitments are undertaken, each Schedule shall specify:

   (a) terms, limitations and conditions on market access;
   (b) conditions and qualifications on national treatment;
   (c) undertakings relating to additional commitments;
   (d) where appropriate the time-frame for implementation of such commitments; and
   (e) the date of entry into force of such commitments.

2.   Measures inconsistent with both Articles XVI and XVII shall be inscribed in the column relating to Article XVI. In this case the inscription will be considered to provide a condition or qualification to Article XVII as well.

3.   Schedules of specific commitments shall be annexed to this Agreement and shall form an integral part thereof.

Article XXI

Modification of Schedules

1.   (a) A Member (referred to in this Article as the "modifying Member") may modify or withdraw any commitment in its Schedule, at any time after three years have elapsed from the date on which that commitment entered into force, in accordance with the provisions of this Article.
   (b) A modifying Member shall notify its intent to modify or withdraw a commitment pursuant to this Article to the Council for Trade in Services no later than three months before the intended date of implementation of the modification or withdrawal.

2.   (a) At the request of any Member the benefits of which under this Agreement may be affected (referred to in this Article as an "affected Member") by a proposed modification or withdrawal notified under subparagraph 1(b), the modifying Member shall enter into negotiations with a view to reaching agreement on any necessary compensatory adjustment. In such negotiations and agreement, the Members concerned shall endeavour to maintain a general level of mutually advantageous commitments not less favourable to trade than that provided for in Schedules of specific commitments prior to such negotiations.
   (b) Compensatory adjustments shall be made on a most-favoured-nation basis.

3.   (a) If agreement is not reached between the modifying Member and any affected Member before the end of the period provided for negotiations, such affected Member may refer the matter to arbitration. Any affected

Member that wishes to enforce a right that it may have to compensation must participate in the arbitration.

(b) If no affected Member has requested arbitration, the modifying Member shall be free to implement the proposed modification or withdrawal.

4. (a) The modifying Member may not modify or withdraw its commitment until it has made compensatory adjustments in conformity with the findings of the arbitration.

(b) If the modifying Member implements its proposed modification or withdrawal and does not comply with the findings of the arbitration, any affected Member that participated in the arbitration may modify or withdraw substantially equivalent benefits in conformity with those findings. Notwithstanding Article II, such a modification or withdrawal may be implemented solely with respect to the modifying Member.

5. The Council for Trade in Services shall establish procedures for rectification or modification of Schedules. Any Member which has modified or withdrawn scheduled commitments under this Article shall modify its Schedule according to such procedures.

PART V
INSTITUTIONAL PROVISIONS

Article XXII

Consultation

1. Each Member shall accord sympathetic consideration to, and shall afford adequate opportunity for, consultation regarding such representations as may be made by any other Member with respect to any matter affecting the operation of this Agreement. The Dispute Settlement Understanding (DSU) shall apply to such consultations.

2. The Council for Trade in Services or the Dispute Settlement Body (DSB) may, at the request of a Member, consult with any Member or Members in respect of any matter for which it has not been possible to find a satisfactory solution through consultation under paragraph 1.

3. A Member may not invoke Article XVII, either under this Article or Article XXIII, with respect to a measure of another Member that falls within the scope of an international agreement between them relating to the avoidance of double taxation. In case of disagreement between Members as to whether a measure falls within the scope of such an agreement between them, it shall be open to either Member to bring this matter before the Council for Trade in Services.[11] The Council shall refer

---

[11] With respect to agreements on the avoidance of double taxation which exist on the date of entry into force of the WTO Agreement, such a matter may be brought before the Council for Trade in Services only with the consent of both parties to such an agreement.

the matter to arbitration. The decision of the arbitrator shall be final and binding on the Members.

Article XXIII

Dispute Settlement and Enforcement

1.   If any Member should consider that any other Member fails to carry out its obligations or specific commitments under this Agreement, it may with a view to reaching a mutually satisfactory resolution of the matter have recourse to the DSU.

2.   If the DSB considers that the circumstances are serious enough to justify such action, it may authorize a Member or Members to suspend the application to any other Member or Members of obligations and specific commitments in accordance with Article 22 of the DSU.

3.   If any Member considers that any benefit it could reasonably have expected to accrue to it under a specific commitment of another Member under Part III of this Agreement is being nullified or impaired as a result of the application of any measure which does not conflict with the provisions of this Agreement, it may have recourse to the DSU. If the measure is determined by the DSB to have nullified or impaired such a benefit, the Member affected shall be entitled to a mutually satisfactory adjustment on the basis of paragraph 2 of Article XXI, which may include the modification or withdrawal of the measure. In the event an agreement cannot be reached between the Members concerned, Article 22 of the DSU shall apply.

Article XXIV

Council for Trade in Services

1.   The Council for Trade in Services shall carry out such functions as may be assigned to it to facilitate the operation of this Agreement and further its objectives. The Council may establish such subsidiary bodies as it considers appropriate for the effective discharge of its functions.

2.   The Council and, unless the Council decides otherwise, its subsidiary bodies shall be open to participation by representatives of all Members.

3.   The Chairman of the Council shall be elected by the Members.

Article XXV

Technical Cooperation

1.   Service suppliers of Members which are in need of such assistance shall have access to the services of contact points referred to in paragraph 2 of Article IV.

2.   Technical assistance to developing countries shall be provided at the multilateral level by the Secretariat and shall be decided upon by the Council for Trade in Services.

Article XXVI

Relationship with Other International Organizations

The General Council shall make appropriate arrangements for consultation and cooperation with the United Nations and its specialized agencies as well as with other intergovernmental organizations concerned with services.

PART VI
FINAL PROVISIONS

Article XXVII

Denial of Benefits

A Member may deny the benefits of this Agreement:

(a) to the supply of a service, if it establishes that the service is supplied from or in the territory of a non-Member or of a Member to which the denying Member does not apply the WTO Agreement;

(b) in the case of the supply of a maritime transport service, if it establishes that the service is supplied:

  (i) by a vessel registered under the laws of a non-Member or of a Member to which the denying Member does not apply the WTO Agreement, and

  (ii) by a person which operates and/or uses the vessel in whole or in part but which is of a non-Member or of a Member to which the denying Member does not apply the WTO Agreement;

(c) to a service supplier that is a juridical person, if it establishes that it is not a service supplier of another Member, or that it is a service supplier of a Member to which the denying Member does not apply the WTO Agreement.

Article XXVIII

Definitions

For the purpose of this Agreement:

(a) "measure" means any measure by a Member, whether in the form of a law, regulation, rule, procedure, decision, administrative action, or any other form;

(b) "supply of a service" includes the production, distribution, marketing, sale and delivery of a service;

(c) "measures by Members affecting trade in services" include measures in respect of

  (i) the purchase, payment or use of a service;

      (ii) the access to and use of, in connection with the supply of a service, services which are required by those Members to be offered to the public generally;

      (iii) the presence, including commercial presence, of persons of a Member for the supply of a service in the territory of another Member;

(d) "commercial presence" means any type of business or professional establishment, including through

     i. the constitution, acquisition or maintenance of a juridical person, or

     ii. the creation or maintenance of a branch or a representative office,

within the territory of a Member for the purpose of supplying a service;

(e) "sector" of a service means,

      (i) with reference to a specific commitment, one or more, or all, subsectors of that service, as specified in a Member's Schedule,

      (ii) otherwise, the whole of that service sector, including all of its subsectors;

(f) "service of another Member" means a service which is supplied,

      (i) from or in the territory of that other Member, or in the case of maritime transport, by a vessel registered under the laws of that other Member, or by a person of that other Member which supplies the service through the operation of a vessel and/or its use in whole or in part; or

      (ii) in the case of the supply of a service through commercial presence or through the presence of natural persons, by a service supplier of that other Member;

(g) "service supplier" means any person that supplies a service;[12]

(h) "monopoly supplier of a service" means any person, public or private, which in the relevant market of the territory of a Member is authorized or established formally or in effect by that Member as the sole supplier of that service;

(i) "service consumer" means any person that receives or uses a service;

(j) "person" means either a natural person or a juridical person;

(k) "natural person of another Member" means a natural person who resides in the territory of that other Member or any other Member, and who under the law of that other Member:

      (i) is a national of that other Member; or

      (ii) has the right of permanent residence in that other Member, in the case of a Member which:

         1. does not have nationals; or

---

[12] Where the service is not supplied directly by a juridical person but through other forms of commercial presence such as a branch or a representative office, the service supplier (i.e. the juridical person) shall, nonetheless, through such presence be accorded the treatment provided for service suppliers under the Agreement. Such treatment shall be extended to the presence through which the service is supplied and need not be extended to any other parts of the supplier located outside the territory where the service is supplied.

2. accords substantially the same treatment to its permanent residents as it does to its nationals in respect of measures affecting trade in services, as notified in its acceptance of or accession to the WTO Agreement, provided that no Member is obligated to accord to such permanent residents treatment more favourable than would be accorded by that other Member to such permanent residents. Such notification shall include the assurance to assume, with respect to those permanent residents, in accordance with its laws and regulations, the same responsibilities that other Member bears with respect to its nationals;

(l) "juridical person" means any legal entity duly constituted or otherwise organized under applicable law, whether for profit or otherwise, and whether privately-owned or governmentally-owned, including any corporation, trust, partnership, joint venture, sole proprietorship or association;

(m) "juridical person of another Member" means a juridical person which is either:

   (i) constituted or otherwise organized under the law of that other Member, and is engaged in substantive business operations in the territory of that Member or any other Member; or

   (ii) in the case of the supply of a service through commercial presence, owned or controlled by:

     1. natural persons of that Member; or

     2. juridical persons of that other Member identified under subparagraph (i);

(n) a juridical person is:

   (i) "owned" by persons of a Member if more than 50 per cent of the equity interest in it is beneficially owned by persons of that Member;

   (ii) "controlled" by persons of a Member if such persons have the power to name a majority of its directors or otherwise to legally direct its actions;

   (iii) "affiliated" with another person when it controls, or is controlled by, that other person; or when it and the other person are both controlled by the same person;

(o) "direct taxes" comprise all taxes on total income, on total capital or on elements of income or of capital, including taxes on gains from the alienation of property, taxes on estates, inheritances and gifts, and taxes on the total amounts of wages or salaries paid by enterprises, as well as taxes on capital appreciation.

Article XXIX

Annexes

The Annexes to this Agreement are an integral part of this Agreement.

ANNEX ON ARTICLE II EXEMPTIONS

Scope

1. This Annex specifies the conditions under which a Member, at the entry into force of this Agreement, is exempted from its obligations under paragraph 1 of Article II.
2. Any new exemptions applied for after the date of entry into force of the WTO Agreement shall be dealt with under paragraph 3 of Article IX of that Agreement.

Review

3. The Council for Trade in Services shall review all exemptions granted for a period of more than 5 years. The first such review shall take place no more than 5 years after the entry into force of the WTO Agreement.
4. The Council for Trade in Services in a review shall:
    (a) examine whether the conditions which created the need for the exemption still prevail; and
    (b) determine the date of any further review.

Termination

5. The exemption of a Member from its obligations under paragraph 1 of Article II of the Agreement with respect to a particular measure terminates on the date provided for in the exemption.
6. In principle, such exemptions should not exceed a period of 10 years. In any event, they shall be subject to negotiation in subsequent trade liberalizing rounds.
7. A Member shall notify the Council for Trade in Services at the termination of the exemption period that the inconsistent measure has been brought into conformity with paragraph 1 of Article II of the Agreement.

Lists of Article II Exemptions

[The agreed lists of exemptions under paragraph 2 of Article II will be annexed here in the treaty copy of the WTO Agreement.]

ANNEX ON MOVEMENT OF NATURAL PERSONS SUPPLYING SERVICES UNDER THE AGREEMENT

1. This Annex applies to measures affecting natural persons who are service suppliers of a Member, and natural persons of a Member who are employed by a service supplier of a Member, in respect of the supply of a service.

2. The Agreement shall not apply to measures affecting natural persons seeking access to the employment market of a Member, nor shall it apply to measures regarding citizenship, residence or employment on a permanent basis.

3. In accordance with Parts III and IV of the Agreement, Members may negotiate specific commitments applying to the movement of all categories of natural persons supplying services under the Agreement. Natural persons covered by a specific

commitment shall be allowed to supply the service in accordance with the terms of that commitment.

4.   The Agreement shall not prevent a Member from applying measures to regulate the entry of natural persons into, or their temporary stay in, its territory, including those measures necessary to protect the integrity of, and to ensure the orderly movement of natural persons across, its borders, provided that such measures are not applied in such a manner as to nullify or impair the benefits accruing to any Member under the terms of a specific commitment.[13]

ANNEX ON AIR TRANSPORT SERVICES

1.   This Annex applies to measures affecting trade in air transport services, whether scheduled or non-scheduled, and ancillary services. It is confirmed that any specific commitment or obligation assumed under this Agreement shall not reduce or affect a Member's obligations under bilateral or multilateral agreements that are in effect on the date of entry into force of the WTO Agreement.

2.   The Agreement, including its dispute settlement procedures, shall not apply to measures affecting:

(a)   traffic rights, however granted; or

(b)   services directly related to the exercise of traffic rights, except as provided in paragraph 3 of this Annex.

3.   The Agreement shall apply to measures affecting:

(a)   aircraft repair and maintenance services;

(b)   the selling and marketing of air transport services;

(c)   computer reservation system (CRS) services.

4.   The dispute settlement procedures of the Agreement may be invoked only where obligations or specific commitments have been assumed by the concerned Members and where dispute settlement procedures in bilateral and other multilateral agreements or arrangements have been exhausted.

5.   The Council for Trade in Services shall review periodically, and at least every five years, developments in the air transport sector and the operation of this Annex with a view to considering the possible further application of the Agreement in this sector.

6.   Definitions:

(a)   "Aircraft repair and maintenance services" mean such activities when undertaken on an aircraft or a part thereof while it is withdrawn from service and do not include so-called line maintenance.

(b)   "Selling and marketing of air transport services" mean opportunities for the air carrier concerned to sell and market freely its air transport services

---

[13] The sole fact of requiring a visa for natural persons of certain Members and not for those of others shall not be regarded as nullifying or impairing benefits under a specific commitment.

including all aspects of marketing such as market research, advertising and distribution. These activities do not include the pricing of air transport services nor the applicable conditions.

(c) "Computer reservation system (CRS) services" mean services provided by computerised systems that contain information about air carriers' schedules, availability, fares and fare rules, through which reservations can be made or tickets may be issued.

(d) "Traffic rights" mean the right for scheduled and non-scheduled services to operate and/or to carry passengers, cargo and mail for remuneration or hire from, to, within, or over the territory of a Member, including points to be served, routes to be operated, types of traffic to be carried, capacity to be provided, tariffs to be charged and their conditions, and criteria for designation of airlines, including such criteria as number, ownership, and control.

ANNEX ON FINANCIAL SERVICES

1. *Scope and Definition*

    (a) This Annex applies to measures affecting the supply of financial services. Reference to the supply of a financial service in this Annex shall mean the supply of a service as defined in paragraph 2 of Article I of the Agreement.

    (b) For the purposes of subparagraph 3(b) of Article I of the Agreement, "services supplied in the exercise of governmental authority" means the following:

        (i) activities conducted by a central bank or monetary authority or by any other public entity in pursuit of monetary or exchange rate policies;

        (ii) activities forming part of a statutory system of social security or public retirement plans; and

        (iii) other activities conducted by a public entity for the account or with the guarantee or using the financial resources of the Government.

    (c) For the purposes of subparagraph 3(b) of Article I of the Agreement, if a Member allows any of the activities referred to in subparagraphs (b)(ii) or (b)(iii) of this paragraph to be conducted by its financial service suppliers in competition with a public entity or a financial service supplier, "services" shall include such activities.

    (d) Subparagraph 3(c) of Article I of the Agreement shall not apply to services covered by this Annex.

2. *Domestic Regulation*

    (a) Notwithstanding any other provisions of the Agreement, a Member shall not be prevented from taking measures for prudential reasons, including for the protection of investors, depositors, policy holders or persons to whom a fiduciary duty is owed by a financial service supplier, or to ensure the integrity and stability of the financial system. Where such measures do not conform with the provisions of the Agreement, they shall not be used as a means of avoiding the Member's commitments or obligations under the Agreement.

(b) Nothing in the Agreement shall be construed to require a Member to disclose information relating to the affairs and accounts of individual customers or any confidential or proprietary information in the possession of public entities.

3. *Recognition*

(a) A Member may recognize prudential measures of any other country in determining how the Member's measures relating to financial services shall be applied. Such recognition, which may be achieved through harmonization or otherwise, may be based upon an agreement or arrangement with the country concerned or may be accorded autonomously.

(b) A Member that is a party to such an agreement or arrangement referred to in subparagraph (a), whether future or existing, shall afford adequate opportunity for other interested Members to negotiate their accession to such agreements or arrangements, or to negotiate comparable ones with it, under circumstances in which there would be equivalent regulation, oversight, implementation of such regulation, and, if appropriate, procedures concerning the sharing of information between the parties to the agreement or arrangement. Where a Member accords recognition autonomously, it shall afford adequate opportunity for any other Member to demonstrate that such circumstances exist.

(c) Where a Member is contemplating according recognition to prudential measures of any other country, paragraph 4(b) of Article VII shall not apply.

4. *Dispute Settlement*

Panels for disputes on prudential issues and other financial matters shall have the necessary expertise relevant to the specific financial service under dispute.

5. *Definitions*

For the purposes of this Annex:

(a) A financial service is any service of a financial nature offered by a financial service supplier of a Member. Financial services include all insurance and insurance-related services, and all banking and other financial services (excluding insurance). Financial services include the following activities:
Insurance and insurance-related services
  (i) Direct insurance (including co-insurance):
   (A) life
   (B) non-life
  (ii) Reinsurance and retrocession;
  (iii) Insurance intermediation, such as brokerage and agency;

(iv) Services auxiliary to insurance, such as consultancy, actuarial, risk assessment and claim settlement services.

Banking and other financial services (excluding insurance)

(v) Acceptance of deposits and other repayable funds from the public;

(vi) Lending of all types, including consumer credit, mortgage credit, factoring and financing of commercial transaction;

(vii) Financial leasing;

(viii) All payment and money transmission services, including credit, charge and debit cards, travellers cheques and bankers drafts;

(ix) Guarantees and commitments;

(x) Trading for own account or for account of customers, whether on an exchange, in an over-the-counter market or otherwise, the following:

(A) money market instruments (including cheques, bills, certificates of deposits);

(B) foreign exchange;

(C) derivative products including, but not limited to, futures and options;

(D) exchange rate and interest rate instruments, including products such as swaps, forward rate agreements;

(E) transferable securities;

(F) other negotiable instruments and financial assets, including bullion.

(xi) Participation in issues of all kinds of securities, including underwriting and placement as agent (whether publicly or privately) and provision of services related to such issues;

(xii) Money broking;

(xiii) Asset management, such as cash or portfolio management, all forms of collective investment management, pension fund management, custodial, depository and trust services;

(xiv) Settlement and clearing services for financial assets, including securities, derivative products, and other negotiable instruments;

(xv) Provision and transfer of financial information, and financial data processing and related software by suppliers of other financial services;

(xvi) Advisory, intermediation and other auxiliary financial services on all the activities listed in subparagraphs (v) through (xv), including credit reference and analysis, investment and portfolio research and advice, advice on acquisitions and on corporate restructuring and strategy.

(b) A financial service supplier means any natural or juridical person of a Member wishing to supply or supplying financial services but the term "financial service supplier" does not include a public entity.

(c) "Public entity" means:

(i) a government, a central bank or a monetary authority, of a Member, or an entity owned or controlled by a Member, that is principally engaged in carrying out governmental functions or activities for governmental purposes, not including an entity principally engaged in supplying financial services on commercial terms; or

(ii) a private entity, performing functions normally performed by a central bank or monetary authority, when exercising those functions.

SECOND ANNEX ON FINANCIAL SERVICES

1. Notwithstanding Article II of the Agreement and paragraphs 1 and 2 of the Annex on Article II Exemptions, a Member may, during a period of 60 days beginning four months after the date of entry into force of the WTO Agreement, list in that Annex measures relating to financial services which are inconsistent with paragraph 1 of Article II of the Agreement.

2. Notwithstanding Article XXI of the Agreement, a Member may, during a period of 60 days beginning four months after the date of entry into force of the WTO Agreement, improve, modify or withdraw all or part of the specific commitments on financial services inscribed in its Schedule.

3. The Council for Trade in Services shall establish any procedures necessary for the application of paragraphs 1 and 2.

ANNEX ON NEGOTIATIONS ON MARITIME TRANSPORT SERVICES

1. Article II and the Annex on Article II Exemptions, including the requirement to list in the Annex any measure inconsistent with most-favoured-nation treatment that a Member will maintain, shall enter into force for international shipping, auxiliary services and access to and use of port facilities only on:

(a) the implementation date to be determined under paragraph 4 of the Ministerial Decision on Negotiations on Maritime Transport Services; or,

(b) should the negotiations not succeed, the date of the final report of the Negotiating Group on Maritime Transport Services provided for in that Decision.

2. Paragraph 1 shall not apply to any specific commitment on maritime transport services which is inscribed in a Member's Schedule.

3. From the conclusion of the negotiations referred to in paragraph 1, and before the implementation date, a Member may improve, modify or withdraw all or part of its specific commitments in this sector without offering compensation, notwithstanding the provisions of Article XXI.

ANNEX ON TELECOMMUNICATIONS

1. *Objectives*

Recognizing the specificities of the telecommunications services sector and, in particular, its dual role as a distinct sector of economic activity and as the underlying transport means for other economic activities, the Members have agreed to the following Annex with the objective of elaborating upon the provisions of the Agreement with respect to measures affecting access to and use of public telecommunications transport networks and services. Accordingly, this Annex provides notes and supplementary provisions to the Agreement.

2. *Scope*

    (a) This Annex shall apply to all measures of a Member that affect access to and use of public telecommunications transport networks and services.[14]

    (b) This Annex shall not apply to measures affecting the cable or broadcast distribution of radio or television programming.

    (c) Nothing in this Annex shall be construed:

        (i) to require a Member to authorize a service supplier of any other Member to establish, construct, acquire, lease, operate, or supply telecommunications transport networks or services, other than as provided for in its Schedule; or

        (ii) to require a Member (or to require a Member to oblige service suppliers under its jurisdiction) to establish, construct, acquire, lease, operate or supply telecommunications transport networks or services not offered to the public generally.

3. *Definitions*

For the purposes of this Annex:

    (a) "Telecommunications" means the transmission and reception of signals by any electromagnetic means.

    (b) "Public telecommunications transport service" means any telecommunications transport service required, explicitly or in effect, by a Member to be offered to the public generally. Such services may include, *inter alia*, telegraph, telephone, telex, and data transmission typically involving the real-time transmission of customer-supplied information between two or more points without any end-to-end change in the form or content of the customer's information.

    (c) "Public telecommunications transport network" means the public telecommunications infrastructure which permits telecommunications between and among defined network termination points.

    (d) "Intra-corporate communications" means telecommunications through which a company communicates within the company or with or among its subsidiaries, branches and, subject to a Member's domestic laws and regulations, affiliates. For these purposes, "subsidiaries", "branches" and, where applicable, "affiliates" shall be as defined by each Member.

---

[14] This paragraph is understood to mean that each Member shall ensure that the obligations of this Annex are applied with respect to suppliers of public telecommunications transport networks and services by whatever measures are necessary.

"Intra-corporate communications" in this Annex excludes commercial or non-commercial services that are supplied to companies that are not related subsidiaries, branches or affiliates, or that are offered to customers or potential customers.

(e) Any reference to a paragraph or subparagraph of this Annex includes all subdivisions thereof.

4. *Transparency*

In the application of Article III of the Agreement, each Member shall ensure that relevant information on conditions affecting access to and use of public telecommunications transport networks and services is publicly available, including: tariffs and other terms and conditions of service; specifications of technical interfaces with such networks and services; information on bodies responsible for the preparation and adoption of standards affecting such access and use; conditions applying to attachment of terminal or other equipment; and notifications, registration or licensing requirements, if any.

5. *Access to and use of Public Telecommunications Transport Networks and Services*

(a) Each Member shall ensure that any service supplier of any other Member is accorded access to and use of public telecommunications transport networks and services on reasonable and non-discriminatory terms and conditions, for the supply of a service included in its Schedule. This obligation shall be applied, inter alia, through paragraphs (b) through (f).[15]

(b) Each Member shall ensure that service suppliers of any other Member have access to and use of any public telecommunications transport network or service offered within or across the border of that Member, including private leased circuits, and to this end shall ensure, subject to paragraphs (e) and (f), that such suppliers are permitted:

(i) to purchase or lease and attach terminal or other equipment which interfaces with the network and which is necessary to supply a supplier's services;

(ii) to interconnect private leased or owned circuits with public telecommunications transport networks and services or with circuits leased or owned by another service supplier; and

(iii) to use operating protocols of the service supplier's choice in the supply of any service, other than as necessary to ensure the availability of telecommunications transport networks and services to the public generally.

---

[15] The term "non-discriminatory" is understood to refer to most-favoured-nation and national treatment as defined in the Agreement, as well as to reflect sector-specific usage of the term to mean "terms and conditions no less favourable than those accorded to any other user of like public telecommunications transport networks or services under like circumstances".

(c) Each Member shall ensure that service suppliers of any other Member may use public telecommunications transport networks and services for the movement of information within and across borders, including for intra-corporate communications of such service suppliers, and for access to information contained in data bases or otherwise stored in machine-readable form in the territory of any Member. Any new or amended measures of a Member significantly affecting such use shall be notified and shall be subject to consultation, in accordance with relevant provisions of the Agreement.

(d) Notwithstanding the preceding paragraph, a Member may take such measures as are necessary to ensure the security and confidentiality of messages, subject to the requirement that such measures are not applied in a manner which would constitute a means of arbitrary or unjustifiable discrimination or a disguised restriction on trade in services.

(e) Each Member shall ensure that no condition is imposed on access to and use of public telecommunications transport networks and services other than as necessary:

    (i) to safeguard the public service responsibilities of suppliers of public telecommunications transport networks and services, in particular their ability to make their networks or services available to the public generally;

    (ii) to protect the technical integrity of public telecommunications transport networks or services; or

    (iii) to ensure that service suppliers of any other Member do not supply services unless permitted pursuant to commitments in the Member's Schedule.

(f) Provided that they satisfy the criteria set out in paragraph (e), conditions for access to and use of public telecommunications transport networks and services may include:

    (i) restrictions on resale or shared use of such services;

    (ii) a requirement to use specified technical interfaces, including interface protocols, for inter-connection with such networks and services;

    (iii) requirements, where necessary, for the inter-operability of such services and to encourage the achievement of the goals set out in paragraph 7(a);

    (iv) type approval of terminal or other equipment which interfaces with the network and technical requirements relating to the attachment of such equipment to such networks;

    (v) restrictions on inter-connection of private leased or owned circuits with such networks or services or with circuits leased or owned by another service supplier; or

    (vi) notification, registration and licensing.

(g) Notwithstanding the preceding paragraphs of this section, a developing country Member may, consistent with its level of development, place reasonable conditions on access to and use of public telecommunications transport networks and services necessary to strengthen its domestic telecommunications infrastructure and service capacity and to increase its participation in international trade in telecommunications services. Such conditions shall be specified in the Member's Schedule.

6. *Technical Cooperation*

(a) Members recognize that an efficient, advanced telecommunications infrastructure in countries, particularly developing countries, is essential to the expansion of their trade in services. To this end, Members endorse and encourage the participation, to the fullest extent practicable, of developed and developing countries and their suppliers of public telecommunications transport networks and services and other entities in the development programmes of international and regional organizations, including the International Telecommunication Union, the United Nations Development Programme, and the International Bank for Reconstruction and Development.

(b) Members shall encourage and support telecommunications cooperation among developing countries at the international, regional and sub-regional levels.

(c) In cooperation with relevant international organizations, Members shall make available, where practicable, to developing countries information with respect to telecommunications services and developments in telecommunications and information technology to assist in strengthening their domestic telecommunications services sector.

(d) Members shall give special consideration to opportunities for the least-developed countries to encourage foreign suppliers of telecommunications services to assist in the transfer of technology, training and other activities that support the development of their telecommunications infrastructure and expansion of their telecommunications services trade.

7. *Relation to International Organizations and Agreements*

(a) Members recognize the importance of international standards for global compatibility and inter-operability of telecommunication networks and services and undertake to promote such standards through the work of relevant international bodies, including the International Telecommunication Union and the International Organization for Standardization.

(b) Members recognize the role played by intergovernmental and non-governmental organizations and agreements in ensuring the efficient operation of domestic and global telecommunications services, in particular the International Telecommunication Union. Members shall make appropriate arrangements, where relevant, for consultation with such organizations on matters arising from the implementation of this Annex.

ANNEX ON NEGOTIATIONS ON BASIC TELECOMMUNICATIONS

1.   Article II and the Annex on Article II Exemptions, including the requirement to list in the Annex any measure inconsistent with most-favoured-nation treatment that a Member will maintain, shall enter into force for basic telecommunications only on:

  (a) the implementation date to be determined under paragraph 5 of the Ministerial Decision on Negotiations on Basic Telecommunications; or,

  (b) should the negotiations not succeed, the date of the final report of the Negotiating Group on Basic Telecommunications provided for in that Decision.

2.   Paragraph 1 shall not apply to any specific commitment on basic telecommunications which is inscribed in a Member's Schedule.

INDEX

13709364R00067

Made in the USA
San Bernardino, CA
02 August 2014